ONE WOMAN'S YEAR

Persephone Book N° 135
Published by Persephone Books Ltd 2019
Reprinted 2024

First published in 1953

Endpapers taken from an early 1950s fabric by
Sheila Bownas © the Sheila Bownas Estate.

Typeset in ITC Baskerville by
KSPM, Wolverhampton

Printed and bound in Germany by
GGP Media GmbH, Poessneck

978 191 0263 259

Persephone Books Ltd
8 Edgar Buildings
Bath BA1 2EE
01225 425050

www.persephonebooks.co.uk

ONE WOMAN'S YEAR

by

STELLA MARTIN CURREY

****

PERSEPHONE BOOKS
BATH

CONTENTS

Contents

Contents

The quotations at the beginning of each month are from Rider's 'British Merlin' 1677

ACKNOWLEDGMENTS

For permission to reprint certain copyright material in this book, thanks are warmly given to :

Miss Marjorie Towers and Messrs Michael Joseph for *Tea with Mr Rochester* ; Miss Stella Gibbons and Messrs Longman, Green & Co. for *Cold Comfort Farm* ; the Editor of *The New English Weekly* for *Angelico Gold*, and the Oxford University Press for *Reconquest*, by R. N. Currey ; the Cresset Press for Frances Cornford's *London Spring* and *After the Examination* ; Miss Kathleen Raine and Messrs Hamish Hamilton for *Worry about Money* ; Miss Kathleen Raine, the Editor of *Penguin New Writing* and Messrs Jonathan Cape for *Mysterious Kor* ; the Hogarth Press for *To the Lighthouse* by Virginia Woolf ; Messrs Constable and Co. for *Letters of Kathleen Mansfield* ; Messrs William Heinemann, Ltd., for Anthony Thorne's *Cabbage Holiday* ; Messrs Macmillan & Co. for *Elizabeth and Her German Garden* ; and the Editor of the Cornhill Magazine for the quotation on page 125 from Osbert Lancaster's *Saracen's Head*.

TO

THE MEMORY

OF

TIRZAH GARWOOD

JANUARY

January. *This is the Season for good husbands to lop and prune superfluous Branches and Fruit trees : Uncover their Roots ; set all kinds of Quick-sets and Fruit trees in the New of the Moon. Be sure that the Wind be not North or East ; and set the same sides to the South and West, which grew at the first. Set Beans, dig Gardens : Drench weak and sick Cattle, Kine, with Verjuice ; Horses with Water and Ground Malt, sodden with a little Bran.*

In this Month let not Blood, nor use physick, unless necessity constrain thee ; beware of taking cold, for Rheums and Plegm do much increase this Moneth : It's hurtful to fast long, to drink White Wine fasting is good. Use Meats that are moderately hot, for the best physick is warm diet, warm Cloaths, good Fires, and a merry, honest Wife.

British Merlin 1677

BOOKS FOR THE FAMILY

JANUARY is an outrageous month. The most you can say for it is that it has the negative virtue of a new exercise book. And as with most exercise books the blots and crossings out begin, if not on the first page, most certainly on the second. After the stern purity of New Year's Day : 'You can't lose your temper today, darling ! ' . . . the blots fall sootily.

But this is a disgruntled estimate, for often in very early January comes a day of serene sun, when you wake to the sound of excited rooks, and a feeling that you could do with a blanket less. Then is the time to go round the garden and be surprised that a number of optimistic bulbs are actually showing, and to send that post-card 'Is it too late for you to let me have the promised white lilac ? '

On such a day Mrs Cartwright, tying on her apron before she has a go at what she calls 'me fireplace,' says to me : 'You can always look around and see others worse off than yourself.' I know then that she is reacting to the promise of a fine day, and that January is not so bad after all.

And there are definite pleasures which belong to the month. One of them I count reading with the family.

Sometimes one hears women say : 'Thank heaven he can put himself to bed now and there's no more of that awful reading.' What a pity that is. Such people are quite capable of adding to their moan that their children will read nothing but comics. There is no need to lose any sleep over comics if the early years of reading, between two and six, have been a real part of the give-and-take between mother and child. By six, if the reading has been reasonably wide and intelligently thought out, the child's taste will be formed, and he can add a certain amount of comic reading to his diet without harm. Comics will never satisfy him completely ; he will quite instinctively look for something better.

'We'll save our *Orlando* and *Babar* books for our own children,' says Roddy, and looking at the battered covers one wonders if they'll make it ; but the idea is sound. I never look at a prim row of Beatrix Potter books without almost smelling bath soap and warm towels and seeing a red mouth rimmed with supper-time milk. 'She walks like Jemima Puddle Duck,' is a family phrase which means something exact to us, and we hardly ever get through a blackberry picnic without somebody quoting out of *Peter Rabbit*, 'Bread and milk and blackberries for supper.' And what a moment of pure joy came to us all when, after a visit to a remote village high up on Exmoor last summer, Roddy rushed to us with some amazing news: 'There's a tailor's shop, and in it a tailor sitting cross-legged on the counter like the man in the *Tailor of Gloucester* ! '

It doesn't matter how young the child is, he always appreciates firmly drawn characters. I remember with gratitude how Alison Uttley's *Sam Pig*; Nancy Catford's *Doctor Maurice the Mouse, M.B.* (' the little animals thought M.B. stood for Much Better '); and the sophisticated urban Puffins *Twink and Waggle* (' I like housework.' 'What is housework ? ') books by Rodney Bennett and Joyce Dennys ; saw us through various infectious diseases.

To the early days belong also *The Toy Town Series* by S. G. Hulme Beaman, *The Twin Books* by Lucy Fitch Perkins and the beautifully illustrated *Pere Castor Books*.

My children have used my own childhood's copies of *Alice in Wonderland* with the Tenniel illustrations, and the *Wind in the Willows* : ' I don't think you ought to have drawn faces in Alice,' says Roddy reprovingly. 'You weren't very good at drawing, were you?' One cannot say anything about these two books, except that I envy anybody introducing either of these to a receptive child for the first time.

If a child does not learn nursery rhymes from his mother or nurse he never learns them, and misses the first step in the appreciation of rhythm and a liking for poetry. Get your small child to like poetry and you've begun shaping his taste in the best way. A war-time anthology of poetry we read over and over again is *A Child's Garland*, collected by Jane Carton. In this the selection is wide and delightful. *The Children's Week-end Book* verse section, the *Dragon Book of Verse* and the collected *Rhymes and Verses* of Walter de la Mare are others which have given our children endless pleasure. The natural taste of children is good, and they respond immediately to wit and colour, and polished style. Roddy, through reading with his father for purest pleasure, greatly appreciates many of the animal poems out of D. H. Lawrence's *Birds, Beasts and Flowers*, likes the whole of *The Flight* by C. Day Lewis and parts of the exciting *Ballad of the Mari Lwyd* by Vernon Watkins. What child wouldn't like that ticking ominous chorus: 'Midnight. Midnight. Midnight. Midnight. Hark at the hands of the clock!'

I would like to put in a plea here that you don't introduce your children to made-easy versions of the classics. I know reading aloud *Uncle Remus* in the Southern American States dialect, for instance, is a bit of an effort, but it is worth it, for half the flavour of the stories is lost if they're translated into dull plain English. And you'll be rewarded by your child's delight in the tumbling humorous phrases and his appreciation of such titles as 'The Laughing Place,' 'The

Moon in the Mill Pond,' 'Who Nibbled up the Butter,' 'Loungin' Around and Sufferin'. This suggestion goes too for *Treasure Island, Kidnapped, Little Women* and *Black Beauty*; *Swiss Family Robinson* and *Robinson Crusoe.* They can all be read aloud neat, round about eight to ten. *Kidnapped* I find is almost more popular than *Treasure Island* if read aloud. Its subtle plot might prove a little difficult for a child on its own, though he would respond with delight to this story of a *boy on his own* if you could put up fingerposts occasionally.

Among the stories of real adventures which have delighted Roddy and Richard most in the last two years have been that superb book on tiger hunting, *The Man-eaters of Kumaon* by Jim Corbett, which more than any other I know gives a sane appreciation of the relative and dignified place of man and animals in the world. Then there is *The Kon-Tiki Expedition* by Thor Heyerdahl, which is unique because it tells you with unforgettable vividness what it is like to live close to the surface of the sea for a long time. The mysterious world of fishes is so much nearer to a raft than a ship. After hearing this read aloud, and then reading it to himself, Roddy, who is ten, made a model of the Kon-Tiki raft and modelled a whale-shark in clay; and when we were at the seaside on a rough day was making yet another raft out of beach wood and straw to show just what must have happened to the Kon-Tiki when it was being beaten up on the reef. The pleasure he has had out of the book is endless.

The Wooden Horse (Eric Williams) and *African Adventures* by Allan K. Taylor (Uncle Jock of Children's Hour) are two others the boys have liked because they were obviously real and exciting.

Once, when I was about nine, I wrote an adventure story about a party of boys and girls who, heaven alone knows how, got down a silver mine in Syria in order to find a fabulous town full of treasures. I remember nothing much about it except that about every ten lines the words ' they sat down to a well-earned meal ' occurred. It is this same comforting insistence as a kettle always on the boil, and a meal about to be produced, which has delighted me during my long apprenticeship to Arthur Ransome. High among the it-might-have-happened-to-me books the boys place *The Otterbury Incident* by C. Day Lewis, *Blue Door Venture* by Pamela Brown and *The Children of One End Street* by Eve Garnett.

I had never read Mark Twain, *The Adventures of Huckleberry Finn* and *Tom Sawyer* properly until I read them aloud to the children, and the same goes for the unforgettable *Moby Dick*. If I ever have grandchildren I shall hope to fill up some more gaps in my education ! I have only shared one Biggles book with Roddy, although he has read the lot, but that one fascinated me because the villain had a set of steel false teeth! Buchan's *Thirty-nine Steps*, *Book of Escapes* and the *Three Hostages* are also very much liked. *Oliver Twist*, the *Christmas Carol*, with Rackham illustrations, and *Great Expectations* are the only Dickens we have read.

I don't know if H. G. Wells's book called *Floor Games* is still in print, but this is a treasure indeed if you can get hold of it. How to create a whole town on the nursery floor is its theme, and because of it many days indoors with coughs and colds have been bearable for us. Inspired by an idea from it the children's grandfather made them a large box of bricks of the $6 \times 1\frac{1}{2}$ variety. These are now polished by years of use. They are in every way the best sort of bricks, large enough to do real building.

Fantasy and fairy tales are an essential part of reading. Whether a child believes in fairies or impossible situations is beside the point. He must have a good mixture in a healthy reading diet. All our favourites have a streak of brutality in them which might not be approved of by those who still cling to the notion that children's stomachs are not strong. *The Adventures of Baron Munchausen* ('most extraordinary adventures which are well worth reader's notice'); *The Hobbit*, by J. R. R. Tolkien; *The Fatty Puffs and Thinifers* by André Maurois; *The Pirates of the Deep Green Sea* by Eric Linklater; *Irish Fairy Tales* by James Stephens, illustrated by Rackham; most parts of *Gulliver*'s *Travels*; and *Pinocchio* have been read and re-read. Fantasy should have humour behind it or it quickly loses piquancy, and all these books have humour as top ingredient. As a result of reading a version of the *Sorcerer's Apprentice*, Richard used a gramophone token to buy Dukas's *L'Apprenti Sorcier*.

Richard has always shown a disposition to begin and go on; Roddy, as second child, is more inclined to begin and stop. Richard practised phonetics diligently when he was learning to read, so much so that Roddy complained: 'I wish you wouldn't do that awful reading.' Roddy practised nothing, but was a trial to all who dealt with him. His attitude till seven was that what he *could* read was not worth reading, and so he washed his hands of the whole affair. He seemed to have no transition stage. One day he could hardly read at all, the next he was starting a whole book—which he finished.

Richard, at twelve to thirteen, was reading *The Cloister and the Hearth*, *The Hunchback of Notre Dame*, *The Three Musketeers* and *Old St Paul's*.

Roddy, three years younger, may or may not acquire the staying power necessary to read books of this length. He has dipped into *Old St Paul's* and was heard horribly chanting: 'My coffins will sell—so what care I! Drink the

Plague ! ' so apparently he has grasped what the book was about. That is all that can, or need, be said.

'*Struwwelpeter*'—the Victorian book of moral rhymes—' Here is cruel Frederick see,' and its witty enchanting son, Hilaire Belloc's *Cautionary Verses* . . . 'Matilda told such dreadful lies. It made one gasp and stretch one's eyes,' and from the *Bad Child's Book of Beasts* : ' What, would you slap the porcupine, unhappy child—desist ! ' What fun lies in these for everybody in the family, not only for the delinquent and unrepentant young !

I've written this from my own experience which means it does not include books especially meant for girls, but from my own childhood I remember that in a family of boys and girls we all read everything. Boys perhaps are more genuinely attracted by practical books of knowledge and workmanship than girls. The series of books, 'Adventure and Discovery,' which include informative articles on such varied subjects as deep sea diving and famous art forgeries, are read by my boys as soon as I can get hold of them. Richard greatly liked Van Loon's *The Home of Mankind*, with drawings in which the facts are presented imaginatively so that geography becomes at once alive—a ship climbing up over a round world's edge, the mountains under the sea.

Having a book on hand which the family is reading is a pleasure which fits ideally into the school holidays. It is not easy to find books which interest a whole circle of say four, five and six people, but it can be done, once the age of the youngest member is between eight and nine. Communal reading provides those rest periods which make for good temper in a set of people who have over a period of weeks to see a lot of each other. It calls for personal effort which television viewing does not, and it is a very useful accomplishment to be able, later in life, to read aloud well, without notice, in public, anything that is handed to you. Recently, remembering how we had enjoyed it as children, we read aloud, strictly in turn, Conan Doyle's *The Lost World*. Once we had skipped the love-interest, conveniently put in at the beginning and afterwards blissfully absent—the excitement of visiting that lost plateau with its monstrous primeval inhabitants gripped us, so much so that when it looked as if the book couldn't be finished before the end of the holidays the last readings took place round the packing of Richard's trunk. 'Of course nowadays you could go there in a plane, or hover in a helicopter and watch the dinosaurs playing underneath,' said Roddy, 'but it wouldn't be so good. Much better to be shut off from help and in terrible danger every minute.'

Radio did not take the place of reading, and, in spite of many pessimistic head shakings, I don't suppose television will either, if in the early years reading has become a pleasure and a necessity. It more or less rests with us.

VISIT TO THE HAIRDRESSER

GOING to the hairdresser after the children have returned to school in January is delightful. Best, if they go away to school, if you can go on the way back from the station when you are feeling low. There is something about pink walls and dove-grey overalls, the flattering way everybody knows just what shampoo you have, and which cubicle you like that restores a little of your wilting self-esteem. After over-concentration on 3 pr. shorts, 3 pr. pants, 6 pr. socks, 12 hanks, it is soothing to be shown hair styles in *Vogue* and to be asked if you wouldn't like to try that amusing short one on the right. You have enough sense to say 'Thank you, no,' but it is delightful to be with those who think it matters a great deal how you look, and you lean over the basin feeling with the first tingling impact of the hot water the stirring of a new optimism.

BURST PIPE

There was a period immediately following the war when adventures with burst pipes seemed more dreadful and more numerous than they have been since. Perhaps it is that since then we have had more men about ; and have therefore learned to concentrate on the intricacies of archaic water systems ; perhaps plumbers are not so elusive and the winters have been less severe. The worst day I remember contained in its chilly circle a period when, while I telephoned for help, my home was entirely taken over by kind neighbours who organised a chain service in the lavatory, where a stream of water hit the wall opposite at a height of about ten feet with the pressure of a powerful fire hose behind it. The only way to stop a pantomime waterfall from rippling down the stairs was for one person to stand on the lavatory seat and hold a large jug which filled in a matter of seconds, another to stand on a pair of steps and seize the jug and substitute an empty one. A third emptied the jug. Efficient readers, and those who live in modern houses, will no doubt be appalled at the Heath Robinson nature of this picture, but when one has been away from home for four years, and the key controlling the main has been mislaid, and the water-works has to cycle to your aid, this sort of thing happens. People who live in Victorian houses should not burst pipes is a good but well-nigh unworkable motto. The water system of three houses being dependent on each other was something invincible Victorians regarded as natural. No doubt they would have had nothing but contempt for a twentieth-century woman who thought the worst job of January was to call two houses on the telephone (if cowardly) or go and knock on two doors (if brave) and say : 'I'm sorry, but we've got a burst pipe, the water will have to be off till the plumber has been.' You know how it is. One says apologetically : 'I've phoned three . . .' One sees the struggle. One's good friends of sunny May and June are reminding themselves that you can't help it, and there but for the grace of, and so on. But in vain.

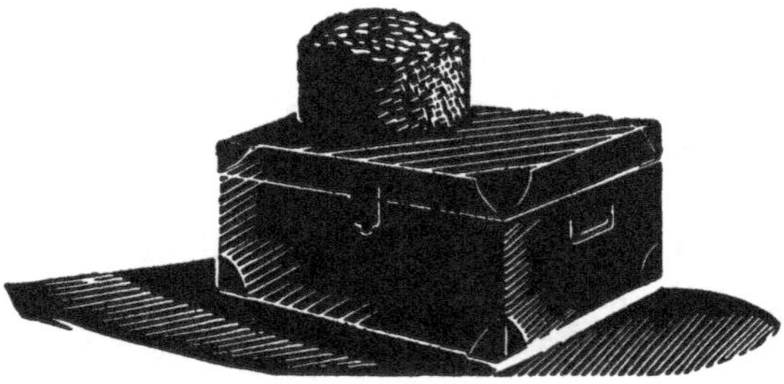

TUCK BOX CAKE

THIS cake which accompanied my brothers and uncles to school and now goes with my son is a plain fruit cake which is economical to make, but doesn't hit you that way when you eat it. I've heard man after man say, ' Good cake, this,' with an air of discovery, as if it is the first time ever. The amounts I give here make two large cakes—cakes big enough to go round a school table. If you want something less wholesale half the amounts will make two ordinary-sized cakes.

Ingredients

2 *lb. Self-raising flour*
½ *lb. Margarine*
2 *Eggs*
2 *teaspoonfuls Mixed spice*
Salt
Nuts for top

1 *lb. Sugar*
½ *lb. Lard*
1½ *lbs. Fruit (can be sultanas and currants, dates, candied peel, cherries)*

Method

Rub fats into flour and add dry ingredients. Add a little milk to beaten eggs and mix thoroughly before adding to mixture. Bake in a moderate oven.

A VISIT TO THE TOWER OF LONDON

I PERSONALLY prefer taking children to London in the Christmas holidays for two main reasons. First the weather, if you pick one of those mild days which are quite common in January except in the really fiercest winters, is suitably cool. Also you have a chance of making the children decide on a play or a pantomime for the afternoon, and this halves the day's exertions for yourself. Usually they won't hear of it. They want to spend *all* day at the Tower.

It is certainly delightful there in winter. You feel much more nearly that the place belongs to you then than in the glare of sunlight with crowds of people making the place one glorified fish queue. How much easier, with a background of grey Thames and sullen shadows underneath that wide and sinister arch, to imagine how those who had arrived at the Tower via the Traitor's Gate must have felt. Up these steps walked Sir Thomas More, Anne Boleyn, Cromwell, Queen Katherine Howard and Lady Jane Gray, and saw in front of them the overpowering bulk of the Bloody Tower.

In winter, too, how delightful to come into the Wakefield Tower, to the guards' glowing fire, and the starry brilliance of the most beautiful jewels in the world. In this beautiful vaulted chamber Henry VI was murdered, and now the beefeater's cat purrs in and out of your legs as you gaze on Queen Victoria's little crown, the Queen's Imperial State crown in which is the ruby given to the Black Prince by Pedro the Cruel, and Queen Elizabeth's Salt, a fabulously beautiful piece of plate. Oliver Cromwell, who is responsible for so much, is responsible, too, for the comparative modernity of most of the regalia. He melted down or sold nearly all the regalia of six centuries of the English monarchy, so not many of the pieces in the Tower are earlier than the seventeenth century.

Children vary in the amount of interest they show in weapons and armour, so the armouries in the White Tower will either take you a few minutes to go through, or hours. With my boys it is hours, with special attention paid to the execution block and axe, and the model of the rack in the Crypt of the Chapel of St John.

Sir Walter Raleigh's little lodging 'here he made the history of the world,' catches at the imagination on a grey day nearly as much as the evocative inscriptions on the walls of the Beauchamp Tower—Robert Dudley . . . Jane . . . and under a bear and a lion supporting a ragged staff . . . John Dudle—died 1554.

On Tower Green a rook, cawing sardonically, walks over the small square plot paved with granite, on which were executed Anne Boleyn, Queen Katherine Howard, Lady Jane Grey, and Robert Devereux Earl of Essex—among others.

'They were all beheaded with an axe, except Queen Anne Boleyn, whose head was cut off with a sword—get off that, can't you ! ' a beefeater tells us and the rook at the same time.

Yes, you want to go to the Tower with children if you haven't been. History is a glowing reality there—the buses crossing Tower Bridge, the wireless sounding from the Bloody Tower are the myths.

JANE EYRE

Mr Rochester, as he sat in his damask-covered chair, looked different to what I had seen him look before ; not quite so stern—much less gloomy. There was a smile on his lips, and his eyes sparkled, whether with wine or not, I am not sure ; but I think it very probable.

He had been looking two minutes at the fire, and I had been looking the same length of time at him, when, turning suddenly, he caught my gaze fastened on his physiognomy.

'You examine me, Miss Eyre,' said he : 'do you think me handsome ?'

I should, if I had deliberated, have replied to this question by something conventionally vague and polite ; but the answer somehow slipped from my tongue before I was aware : 'No, Sir.'

'Ah ! By my word ! there is something singular about you,' said he : 'you have the air of a little nonnette ; quaint, quiet, grave and simple, as you sit with your hands before you, and your eyes generally bent on the carpet (except, by-the-by, when they are directed piercingly to my face ; as just now, for instance) ; and when one asks you a question, or makes a remark to which you are obliged to reply, you rap out a round rejoinder, which, if not blunt, is at least brusque. What do you mean by it ?'

'Sir, I was too plain : I beg your pardon. I ought to have replied that it was not easy to give an impromptu answer to a question about appearances ; that tastes differ ; that beauty is of little consequence, or something of that sort.'

'You ought to have replied no such thing. Beauty of little consequence, indeed ! And so, under pretence of softening the previous outrage, of stroking and soothing me into placidity, you stick a sly penknife under my ear ! Go on : what fault do you find with me, pray ? I suppose I have all my limbs and all my features like any other man ? '

' Mr Rochester, allow me to disown my first answer : I intended no pointed repartee : it was only a blunder.'

' Just so : I think so : and you shall be answerable for it. Criticise me : does my forehead not please you ? '

He lifted up the sable waves of hair which lay horizontally over his brow, and showed a solid enough mass of intellectual organs, but an abrupt deficiency where the suave sign of benevolence should have risen.

CHARLOTTE BRONTË

TEA WITH MR ROCHESTER

PRISSY hovered in the background. She had time to see, before Aunt Athene called attention to her presence, that this was not the drawing-room of snow and fire that had so captivated Jane Eyre ; but a sombre book-lined room with chairs of red-and-gold leather. Then, as if she were crossing a vast stage into a pool of limelight, she came forward, stepping from Persian rug to rug, to take the hand held out to her. But he was still talking to Aunt Athene and shook hands with Prissy without looking at her. His hand was so cold it gave one a fresh feeling, as of gathering snowdrops in a frosty wood.

They were too much interested in their conversation to be aware of her for a long time. She sat on a slippery sofa with elegant golden feet, and drank in everything.

It was a very interesting conversation. Prissy tried to remember every word of it to record in her diary. She was very proud that a relation of hers could evoke the sudden delighted laughter that made Mr Considine wrinkle up his eyes. She was proud of Aunt Athene's beauty, her wit, her tea-rose quality.

But suddenly Mr Considine took her by surprise. The blue eyes looked straight into her own, and he said, with an amused smile :

'Prissy has been weighing me all this time in her invisible scales. And what, Prissy, if I may ask so personal a question, is your private opinion of me ?'

Prissy gave a little gasp. It was a supreme moment. Something must be said—something original, extraordinary. Jane would have known. Oh, for words—words telling, arresting enough. They came, quicker than thought, from she knew not where, in her clear piping treble.

'I *think*, Mr Considine,' she said, brightly and confidingly out of the innocence of her heart, 'that you are more knave than fool.'

FRANCES TOWERS

FEBRUARY

February. *This Month set, cut, and lay Quick-sets and Roses as all other Plants. Set and Plant Vines, Hops, and all fruit that grows on bushes. Sow Pease, Beans, and Onions, furnish your Gardens with Sallads and Pot Herbs for Summer ; Prune and trim all sorts of Fruit trees from Moss, Canker, and superfluous Branches.*

Remove Grafts or young Trees in the last quarter, the Moon being in Aries, Libra, or Scorpio. If necessity urge, you may let Blood but be sparing in Physick, and be sure when a warm day comes to prevent taking of cold through carelessness, for the warm Air this Moneth is not lasting, but oft deceives us to our prejudice.

In this Moneth, slimy Fish, Milk, and the like, that do opilate and stop the Liver, and the Veins, and thicken the Blood, are to be eschued as Enemies to Health. **British Merlin 1677**

EGGS

THE light lasts past tea-time in February, and because of that there comes a day sometimes when it is possible to achieve a mixture of firelight, daffodils, open windows and tea. Delectable. If to this is added an optimistic bird singing outside, and the people sitting round the fire know each other well enough to be able to sit back and say little if they feel like it, then one can forgive February for everything. For about half an hour it can be my favourite month. In the tree alphabet used by the Druids—the quickbeam, or rowan, or mountain ash was the tree of the month. This was a tree they considered good against lightning and against witches' charms, and it was the tree of quickening. Here we come to eggs. If I add eggs to the mixture mentioned above the effect is spoilt, but I seem to share with the Greeks the strong feeling that this month, particularly, is connected with eggs. They considered this the time when the egg of the year was waiting to be hatched out, and represented it by the Greek character Omega—the great O, or egg. Although I know no Greek at all, this seems a sensible symbol to adopt.

It is usually in February that I make a vow that I'm going to learn how to boil an egg properly. So far it has always seemed to me to be one of those devastatingly simple things which is almost impossible to do well. I suppose this desire to improve stirs in February because it is then that hens begin to justify their existence, and altogether one becomes egg-conscious again. What I have said about the Greeks and the Druids hints at deep primitive instincts behind all this, and they were no doubt right. I may have some kink which prevents me from boiling eggs satisfactorily, but judging by the number of egg-boiling aids which have been thought out during the centuries the disability is not new.

This is the sort of thing that happens. I remember the occasion well, for it illustrates exactly what I am trying to say.

My record as a boiler of eggs is thoroughly bad, but when during one February I received from the country a dozen large brown eggs—I always think of such eggs as being sunburnt—I decided to rub all that out.

'It would be a crime to do anything with eggs like these,' I said, 'except boil them.'

'It would be a crime to boil them *hard*!' said my husband Charles.

Now I don't in the least blame him for this reaction, for Charles has been, throughout our married life, extremely forbearing about the way in which our eggs have been boiled. He has never, for instance, said to me as so many men smugly do: 'I don't know anything about cooking, but I *can* boil an egg!' He has never stood beside me at the stove as I heard of one husband doing—and said with a kind of patient fury: 'Look, there's the pan, there's the water and there's the egg. Now, *can* you tell the time!'

Of course men who take this high-handed attitude not only ought to be killed by a thunderbolt as they stand at the stove, but they have obviously never had to produce, as I have more than once been asked to do, one lightly boiled, one picnic-or-near-hard egg, and one neither slip-sloppy-nor-hard-but-something-in-between, all out of the same pan. Somehow I have no deep feelings about boiled eggs personally, and no doubt this is the trouble.

Returning to this particular dozen I am talking about,

I was so determined that for once we should all have perfectly boiled eggs for breakfast that I made the toast and the coffee before putting the eggs into boiling water. This way I felt I could concentrate. While I was making the toast Charles visited the kitchen and informed me that musical people swore by the Overture to the 'Marriage of Figaro' as an egg-boiling aid. It took, he said, three and a half minutes if played correctly, and four if played badly.

I asked if that meant a small permanent orchestra living in the kitchen, or did you hire people to come in specially, or was he just talking about a good gramophone record. Charles said that for the way he liked an egg one had to count an extra thirty after the record was finished—that's if it was a good record.

I feel I am not nearly musical enough for this method.

On the other hand I remembered Mrs Cartwright said she always sings three verses of 'Widdicombe Fair' for a soft boil and four for a harder boil. The difficulty about this is that I don't really know 'Widdicombe Fair.' I never get past Peter Gurney, and there I have to relapse into humming, which would alter the timing.

Before he went upstairs again Charles said that he remembered a magistrate telling him once that suspected mental defectives were always tested by being asked how to boil an egg.

The thoughtful way he said this seemed, at that time in the morning, almost too much.

'If at any time,' I said, 'you wish to get rid of me that would be a simple and painless way.'

Charles had scarcely disappeared before Richard, who was still at home then, asked if I would hear his French verbs while I was getting breakfast ready. I told him that

I would hear them while I was laying the table, but as soon as I began to boil the eggs I would stop.

Roddy, who has an uncanny way of sensing when he thinks I am about to boil over and with a great display of thoughtfulness removes himself from my sight, said he thought it was about time the terrier, Whack, was brushed, and he would go into the garden and do it.

Having disposed of the verbs, Roddy and the dog, I felt success with the eggs was practically assured, but after our conversation you would have thought Charles could have refrained from calling to say that he couldn't find the particular shirt he wanted in the airing cupboard.

At the precise moment I was about to slip the eggs into the boiling water Richard asked me :

'Can I open a packet of oats for the white mice ? And is this it ?' I removed a packet of rice from his grasp and gave him the right one. Understand I had noted the exact time at which the water had started to boil again.

Out of a corner of my eye I saw Whack come in from the garden and go to the pantry door. I ignored him.

It seems unbelievable, but at that moment the window cleaner, who had been unaccountably absent for weeks, chose to pay me a visit, and, with the air of a cheerful prodigal, to rap on the back door. I ignored him too.

I had the spoon poised over the pan to lift out Charles's egg when I heard Roddy's voice behind me.

'It's rather a good thing in a way,' Roddy was saying.

'What's a good thing ?' I asked, still glaring at my watch.

'That I fell out of the laburnum tree,' said Roddy. 'Those teeth were loose anyway.'

Roddy's nose and forehead and shirt were liberally

dabbled with blood, and he held out two gory morsels for me to look at with a placatory air.

I sent Roddy to find a clean shirt, and noticed resignedly that the eggs were still boiling on the stove.

Once more I was convinced of the utter impossibility of boiling eggs.

I may not be good at boiling them, but I am good enough at preserving eggs, if I get the chance, which reminds me of a friend whose husband hurled a large crusty loaf in to the earthenware crock of eggs in waterglass solution under the impression that he was putting the bread away. The splendid distinctiveness of this action ranks with that day of glorious memory, soon after the war, when towards the end of February we had been out to tea at a farm, and been given as a present two dozen new-laid eggs. One of the party, just out of the Army, said as he got into the back of the car, 'Couldn't we have a really large omelette tonight ?' As he sat down heavily there was an unmistakable sound. No doubt Laurel and Hardy, who are used to this sort of thing, would have regarded that crunch as all in the day's work, but we are less used to slapstick. A corner of rug had been flipped accidentally over the bag of eggs, so that they were invisible and the omelette was as was as good as made. Have you ever tried to clear out two dozen eggs from a car seat ?

Do you have egg fights in your family ? This is less spectacular than it sounds. It does not mean throwing eggs at each other, which would be delightful, though ruinous to clothes, but merely in making the empty egg shells into battering-rams, holding them firmly in their cups and ramming the unbroken end against your neighbour's egg-shell. The victor of the table is christened and remains hardening nicely in a cupboard till the next meal. We had one invincible egg called 'The Great White South,' which beat all comers until the day when the cupboard was being spring-cleaned and Mrs Cartwright, sharing with the Romans a healthy dislike for all unbroken shells, cast it into the dustbin.

The Romans, so I learn from the *Golden Bough*, used immediately to break the shells of eggs—and snails—which they had eaten in order to prevent enemies from making magic with them. They had a strong feeling that remains of food were specially vulnerable to magic. It seems a chancy way of poisoning, but they believed poisoning worked that way. Ill-wish half an egg and the ill will fly to the eaten half, and soon that would be one Roman less. Anthropologists suggest that the common practice still observed among us of breaking egg-shells after they have been eaten may well have originated in the same superstition. As far as I am concerned I merely like the sound and sensation of breaking egg-shells, but here again I may be blinding myself to an essential truth.

Wishing to learn more about eggs, I looked up EGG in the *Encyclopaedia Britannica*, and found about four closely printed pages set between EGG, Augustus Leopold, English Painter and EGHAM, town in Surrey. The *E.B.* had a great deal to say about the laying of eggs by snakes and hens, the indigestibility of long-boiled eggs, agreeing here with Charles, the coddling of eggs, and the number of eggs we import and export. It did not, however, tell me, which I regard as far more interesting, that the shells of eggs are formed by a sort of spinning process inside the hen, and that if, injudiciously, you give a hen a fright while this process is going on, it immediately stops spinning, and the hen suffers from acute discomfort. I can well believe it.

But when all has been said the chief fact about eggs is

that when you have a good supply of them you can cook —properly. You can use recipes instead of reading them like fairy stories.

Have you ever tried poaching eggs in wine ? You start this beautiful dream by frying some onions in butter, and then pouring over them some good white wine. Add what herbs you most like, and when they have boiled for a little in the wine break your eggs one by one into the pan. When they are poached remove them, pour the wine through a sieve, put it back into the pan, and thicken with flour and melted butter. It takes about five minutes for the sauce to thicken, and then you spread it over the eggs. About as like ordinary poached eggs as nylons are like woollen stockings.

I remember once eating an omelette with Charles in a Swiss inn. The inn was brown wood inside and out, and the people in it might have been sturdily carved out of brown wood too. The omelette was golden, and about as big as a whale.

I wonder if it could have been made from this recipe.

Take six eggs, and beat the whites to a stiff froth. Mix with the yolks, season, add a spoonful of cream, and a clove of garlic very finely chopped. Fry with infinite slowness in fresh oil.

Yes, when you have eggs you can cook.

PICKING THE FIRST WILD DAFFODILS

EVERY year, in February, I hope I may be again where I once was, gathering the first wild daffodils in the West country. The spring comes earlier there than in most places, and the grey-green spikes and pale golden trumpets are quite often doing their well-known dancing and fluttering act before March comes in. When I last did this it was an afternoon of rain-washed clearness, when the sky was not really blue, but, near the skyline, a luminous duck-egg green. The little orchard where the daffodils were was tip-tilted to the south. Everything there—apple trees, daffodils and blackberry bushes—grew at an angle of forty-five degrees to the road in the valley. ‘Yes, gather what you like,’ the owner of the daffodils had said, and I had a feeling of limitless riches. It has always seemed to me that to be able to give flowers away, not just a little bunch, but whole sheaves of them, a whole yellow orchard floor of them, must be pure joy. I still remember the details of that afternoon, the sound that is made by the leaves and stems of daffodils rubbing together, almost like the creaking of good leather, and the sharp green of the calyxes before they turn yellow, the brittle snap of the hollow flower stems when you break them. And afterwards, going home by the brook, the unexpected sight of a bush of catkins so fluffy that you almost thought ' Persian pussy willow.' At once it was obvious that no box of wild daffodils would be complete without some branches of this. The stream was very high, sliding along in the busy self-absorbed mood which it would lose later when it slowed to mirror the sky. Picking the willow was difficult, but exhilarating, and how pleasant to think of it rushing across England to the blue and white china bowls, the pewter jugs and glasses of town friends. As I went down the lane I was surprised to find that it was already nearly dark, and the duck-egg green had faded to pale lemon.

Picking the catkins had taken much longer than I thought. It would be unbearable if the daffodils did not get away by the evening post. I went into the village post office to hear what would be the latest time for posting the parcels. ' You wrap them up,' said the post-mistress in her warm soft voice, ' and give them to Tom when he passes the end of your lane at five past. That'll save you hurrying, and I'll stamp them when he gets here. They'll be in London by morning, never fear.' Even if she had told me that by special arrangements made by the post office the flowers would be in London at eight o'clock the same evening I would have gratefully believed her. Her comforting voice, the stars just pricking through above the hills, the pollen on my coat sleeve, and the rustling of the daffodils in the big basket were all part of the one delightful fact. Winter was over.

BUYING FRIAR'S BALSAM

> ' In February it is our rule,
> One girl in bed, and one at school.'
>
> Ogden Nash

THERE may have been more fragrant and inspiring poetic statements, but none which goes home to a mother of a family with more conviction. At one period, when my children were still near enough to whooping cough to have susceptible larynxes, buying Friar's Balsam in February used to be a routine event. We even had a jug—a fat white one we called the Friar, kept solely for the purpose of inhaling. What a job it is, making a child inhale.

' Now we'll make a tent over your head with the towel ! '

' But it's hot and steaming in here. It *cooks* me ! '

' That's what it's for, darling. Now breathe hard, pull it in, shut your mouth, breathe out like a horse. Do it four times and then rest.'

' Will you read to me while I do it ? '

' No. I'm counting your breaths.'

' Well, read to me while I rest.'

You know the way it goes. And when it's over and the last drink of water is given, and the last goodnight said, you totter downstairs, exhausted, only to remember that you haven't washed the jug, and that the repellent yellow stain is by now no doubt rimming the thing for ever.

At this time of the year I always remember, too, a paragraph in a seventeenth-century book of simples.

'Take a pint of milk, boyle in it one large onion. At night take out your onion, and put thereto two or three spoonsful of rosewater, sweeten with honey of roses, and drink it warme in your bed. Let your husband drink it three nights together, forbearing supper. *PROBATUM.*'

I should think three nights of that would cure anybody of anything !

PANCAKE PAGODA

THIS is what I call a despair recipe ! One of those which arrives after you have gazed into your pantry and seen such gloomy trifles as one egg, a dish of cold potatoes, a sausage or two, or perhaps some cold meat, and behind you voices in varying keys say they want something savoury and they want a lot of it, and they hope it won't be too long. The thing to do is to use your imagination and blow the washing-up, i.e. don't economise on pans.

First make a pancake batter.

Ingredients for batter

4 *oz. Flour*	*Pinch of salt*
1 *Egg*	*Milk, plus one teaspoonful of water*

(If you have a lot of people to feed these amounts should be doubled, of course.) Let the batter stand for a little, while you set any cold vegetables you have to fry slowly. Add a little thyme to these if you like the slightly exotic flavour the herb gives. This is the bottom layer. The next two layers depend on what you can find. A third pan could contain a curry, and if you decide on this do remember to put the curry powder in as early as you can—while the left-over meat is frying and not at the last minute as so many English cooks do. This could be quite a simple curry with onion, apple or tomato. If you don't like curry then the second layer could be bottled shrimps or left-over fish in a good white sauce, or devilled sausages. The top layer can be either plain tomatoes fried, or mushrooms, if you happen to have any, or raw celery chopped up finely with raw apple and nuts and a slightly sharp dressing.

The idea, having let yourself go and collected about four saucepans or bowls with savoury concoctions in them, is to assemble the whole thing—quickly—into an attractive whole.

Place one pancake on serving dish and pile on to this the fried vegetables. On this place the second pancake covered with curry or fish, or sliced sausages. Cover this with a third, and a top layer of mushrooms or tomato, or celery. Top with final pancake. It is pleasant, of course, if the pancakes can get smaller as they go up, but not necessary. Decorate with green salad. Serve very hot, and cut like a cake into triangular wedges.

CARRYING YOUR HOBBY A STAGE FURTHER

It is very easy to forget when you take children to museums, and there is no doubt they love to go, that the event can be of real value to you personally. A dreary walk round, concentrating on spears, large (carefully mended) jars, and lead coffins not only lowers the spirits, but tires the feet and makes the eyes ache. Indiscriminate looking is quite the worst thing. With very young children I believe in concentrating on one object and having looked a very long time at that, usually far too long for you, to go firmly away. At one time our goal was always a model of a Roman ship unloading grain at a quayside, with models of houses and animals, and all the local notices on the warehouse doors printed in Latin, and the huge steering oar visible through what looked like real swan-dotted water.

Of course if you live near the Victoria and Albert Museum in Kensington, I cannot tell you anything you do not already know about the enchanting collection of dolls' houses and dolls to be seen there. But if you do not know them please go to see them. They will take you or any children you take a whole afternoon to look at, and afterwards you can buy, for a shilling, a beautiful book which illustrates many of the loveliest.

Our local museum's dolls' house, the contents of which took one family thirty years to collect, was for quite a long time a goal for an afternoon walk. Gazing at those tiny crowded rooms I sense with more reality than in any other way the decorous domestic activity of the Victorian age. The nursery under the eaves was bursting with babies, there were five of assorted sizes, with their clothes airing before the fire. On the next floor the lady of the house was just recovering from yet another confinement, and sitting up in a red-and-white wrapper drinking a mug of milk. The new baby was in a cradle, and there was a nurse by her side, and another coming through the door with a can of water. These interesting experiences were obviously a closed book to the young ladies in the drawing-room who, in evening dress, were waiting to take coffee from the egg-shell china coffee service. The gentlemen in the dining-room had got absolutely stuck round their table set with real Bristol glass. Things were fairly quiet in the kitchen, but in the lull between the serving and the washing-up a maid had decided to scrub the floor—slightly hampered by a large basket of eggs and three cats. The mantelpiece was covered with pewter, and the dresser with willow pattern. If the inside of the house was active what shall I say about the outside ? In a corner of the garden, ladies and babies tried out various swings, while on a tennis court of improbable green a set was being played by four ladies in feathered hats. Next to this, an elderly relative in a bath chair was watching a game of croquet. Round a pond, crowded with swans, a gentleman cycled on a penny-farthing, brushing aside a countryman who was trying to sell him two pigeons. This is without going into the feverish activity round the stables.

A visit to the National Science Museum is, as Richard said, 'Nearly as good as a visit to a fun fair, but free.' If your children are old enough you can leave them here for an hour, being quite sure that they will be rapturously occupied with working models, and you can go and have tea in the museum restaurant, or go and look at the embroidery tapestry or china in the Victoria and Albert across the road. If they are not old enough then you'll find you like the National Science Museum very much yourself.

And on most days there is an hour's show of documentary films at the Imperial Institute Cinema (very near to the National Science Museum), again free, where you can insist on everybody sitting down for an hour to recover.

These national museums, of course, are not within the reach of everybody, but most people live within walking, or driving, distance of a local museum or library. Everybody seems to feel that a museum is public property, but less firmly that a reference library belongs to them too. Again the reference library can be used by you and the children for an excursion on a rainy day. If you are interested in old china, glass or embroidery, or art, modelling, gardening, sailing, architecture, music in however elementary a fashion, the books you want to stimulate your interest and give you fresh ideas are there. The children (if they have clean hands and are willing, for say half an hour, to keep quiet) can look at books of rare pictures and begin early, to realise that the reference library is there not only for students, but to make life generally more worth living. Once, when I had four children on my hands, ages from eight to twelve, and the day was incurably rainy and dull, we all put on mackintoshes, walked into the town, and went to the reference library. One child looked at a book of views of castles from the air, another a book of plates on the art of Walt Disney, another joined me in looking at a book of Lowestoft china, and the fourth remained engrossed in a book on the painting of animals.

And sometimes you are lucky enough to see very rare old books. Once you start on these you never know what you are going to find.

I came across this one day :

Fourteenth Century claim for Breach of Promise

For her arrayment, gowns etc.	20	0	0
For the arrayment of her servant	6	13	4
Expenses in time of sickness caused by his unkindness	13	13	0
Expenses seeking him in London, and trying to speak to him	27	16	0
Expenses in the courts in London, tarrying to speak with him at his own request	48	10	0
	£116	12	4

When my children first asked me what rates were for, I told them to keep the dolls' house clean in the museum, to buy more books for the library and to keep the cherry tree pruned in the road outside our house. 'And to pay the man who goes round with the sort of vacuum cleaner for drains,' said Roddy. Anyway, he'd got the idea.

WOMEN

14 Two first seven years, for a rod they doe whine.
28 Two next, as a perle in the world they doe shine.
42 Two next, trim beaute beginneth to swerve.
56 Two next, for matrones or drudges they serve.
70 Two next, doth crave a staffe for a stay.
84 Two next, a beere to fetch them away.

ANON.

A Lesson

Then purchase sane pelfe,
by fiftie and three,
or buckle thy selfe
a drudge for to bee.

THOMAS TUSSER, 1531

EMMA

'I WAS going to observe, sir,' said Frank Churchill, 'that one of the great recommendations of this change would be the very little danger of anybody's catching cold—so much less danger at the Crown than at Randall's! Mr Perry might have reason to regret the alteration, but nobody else could.'

'Sir,' said Mr Woodhouse, rather warmly, 'you are very much mistaken if you suppose Mr Perry to be that sort of character. Mr Perry is extremely concerned when any of us are ill. But I do not understand how the room at the Crown can be safer for you than your father's house.'

'From the very circumstance of its being larger, sir. We shall have no occasion to open the windows at all—not once the whole evening ; and it is that dreadful habit of opening the windows, letting in cold air upon heated bodies, which (as you well know, sir) does the mischief.'

'Open the windows ! but surely, Mr Churchill, nobody could be so imprudent ! I never heard of such a thing. Dancing with open windows ! I am sure neither your father nor Mrs Weston (poor Miss Taylor that was) would suffer it.'

'Ah ! sir—but a thoughtless young person will sometimes step behind a window curtain, and throw up a sash, without it being suspected. I have often known it done myself.'

'Have you, indeed sir ? Bless me ! I never could have supposed it. But I live out of the world, am often astonished at what I hear ! . . .

JANE AUSTEN

March

March. *Now regarding the Wind and Weather, Graft, cut Quick-sets, cover Roots of Fruit trees (opened in December and January) with fat Earth ; sow Oats, Barley, Parsnips, Onions, Carrots, Melons, Cowcumbers, and all kind of Pot-Herbs, slip Hartichoaks and Sage and sow all manner of Garden Seeds.*

Now advise with the honest and able Astrological Physitian ; it is good to purge and let Blood, for in this Moneth the Humors and Blood Increase and gross Feeding breedeth gross Blood and Humors ; therefore use Meats of good digestion, and such as afford good Juice and Nutriment to the Body ; forbear all things salt and purge the Blood by Potions and Blood-letting : Sweetmeats and Drink are commendable. Be sure to eat in the morning before you drink.

British *Merlin* 1677

HOW NOT TO RENOVATE A LAWN

A YEAR or so ago our lawn, which is a town lawn and therefore struggling with hereditary disadvantages, showed signs of becoming bald, not in patches, but all over. March being the month, so my gardening books say, for doing something about this, Charles roused me from what he called my slothful attitude on the subject, and said we must now renovate the lawn.

'Damp, warm weather,' said Charles, looking out into a sort of pale lilac fog, 'ideal for planting grass seed. Have we got any ?'

Of course we hadn't got any, but he rang up a seed merchant, who said he had forty-six customers to supply before the week-end with grass seed, but he hoped to be able to fit Charles's modest order in. Everybody else seemed to be putting acres under grass. Mr Madge, the greengrocer, who is by way of being a better philosopher and orator than a greengrocer, also promised Roddy, who is a friend of his, to let him have two pounds of last year's seed very cheaply. 'It might not come up, but there again it might,' he said, 'anyway it's a bargain at the price.'

While we were waiting for the showers of grass seed to fall upon us we put ropes round the worst part of the lawn, and tried to train Whack not to jump over it.

That afternoon, while we were still waiting, Charles brought in a man who was introduced to me as 'Mr Bates-who-knows-a-great-deal-about-grass. He has very kindly offered to give us advice about our lawn,' said Charles.

Mr Bates, who at once reminded me of Badger in *The Wind in the Willows*, was dark and wise and utterly inscrutable. We took him out into the garden to view the lawn. It was a great pity that I had had no notice of his arrival, for the lawn was really looking at its worst. The two boys, plus two of their friends, two bikes, Whack, a tent and a collection of planks and boards were scattered over it.

Mr Bates shook his head, and said nothing, while Charles and I cleared boys and tents and bikes on to the path.

'Um,' said Mr Bates, and went into a trance.

We looked at him apologetically every few seconds, feeling that our poor stretch of grass was really hardly worthy of such concentration. The solemnity of the occasion even overcame the boys, who dealt severely with Whack, who, showing an utter lack of responsibility, tried to run after a cat.

'Well,' said Mr Bates at last, 'if the lawn is dug over to a depth of two feet, and reduced to a fine tilth—while you are about it I should fell that laburnum tree—and covered all over with strands of black cotton, and kept watered and rolled, you might, in two years, have the beginning of a decent lawn.'

'Can't we go on to the lawn for two years? How do we keep Whack off the lawn for two years?' asked Roddy.

Mr Bates looked at Whack.

'If you keep a dog you must accept the consequences,' he said.

I said I would go and get some tea, and left them to go on talking about it.

After Mr Bates, still looking extremely gloomy, had left I said:

'If we are going to cut down the trees, and reduce everything to a fine tilth, we had better start, hadn't we?'

Charles laughed.

'Good heavens, you don't take all that stuff seriously!'

he said. 'He's a bachelor. He's got time for everything. We've got to improvise. Keeping the children and Whack off the lawn for a week or two will be our chief worry.'

As the grass seed didn't turn up for a few days I managed to forget the lawn, but this was only a short respite. One afternoon, while I was talking to friends in the sitting-room, a large toil-worn hand was suddenly thrust through the open French window. It held a small dirty bag, and a well-known voice said: 'Two shillings—shall I put it on the bill? It's a good two bob's worth, that.'

It was Mr Madge with the cheap line in grass seed.

An hour later a lorry arrived with what looked like half a hundredweight of grass seed. There was, I felt, no chance of escape now. All the materials were at hand. The lawn *must* be renovated.

No instructions were given with the big bag. Obviously the feeling was that anybody who wanted so much of anything knew just what to do with it. Mr Madge's bag, under a layer of what looked like porridge oats which had been mixed with treacle, was covered with instructions.

'When renovating lawn Rake with Judgment, remove weeds and destroy worms.' After tea that day we all did a little raking with judgment, and the result was that in about ten minutes our rakes were full of well-grown roots of grass we could not afford to lose.

Next day rain fell heavily, and Charles said that this was ideal weather for grass planting. We must make the most of it. We put on mackintoshes, and with the rain dripping down our necks, raked some more. Then we sent Richard to the tool shed for stakes and a mallet. As he reached it Roddy came out of it, saying that he could not understand how he had managed to spill half the grass seed out of the bag on to the tool-shed floor. He had only cut a few stitches in the top of the bag so as to be ready when we wanted the seed.

While we were making appropriate exclamations Richard came out of the shed with a tin of black varnish to ask us if we knew we had this. Charles said he thought he'd sent Richard to fetch mallet and stakes, and why was it that nowadays children could not obey the simplest order.

I went on with some raking while Charles and Richard hammered stakes in round the lawn. Of course we all loved sowing the seed, but that delectable job was soon over, and the next stage, tying strands of black cotton to the stakes, was maddening. The lawn which had always seemed rather too small seemed to expand as we tripped over the cotton, broke strands and controlled our tempers with difficulty.

'No hope of keeping birds off without it,' said Charles.

Almost as he spoke a robin flew down under some strands of black cotton, ate his fill of seed, flew up, easily avoiding the strands on the way, perched on the laburnum and burst into grateful song.

Charles and I looked at each other.

Until the boys went to bed the house rang with wild shouts as one or other of them saw a bird negotiating the black cotton. When they were in bed they could not sleep because the wind rose, and the bell Richard had arranged in the pear tree tinkled more than efficiently.

Richard appeared in the sitting-room doorway to ask if I knew if owls ate grass seed, and did I think it would be a good question for Nature Parliament. I said I didn't know, and I thought it would be, and if I heard or saw him again that night something unspeakable would happen.

At midnight Charles said he didn't think that Whack ought to be let out into the garden alone, as he didn't seem to understand about keeping off the lawn.

I went upstairs, and from the bathroom was aware of a good deal of confused noise in the moonlit garden.

'That dog! ' said Charles when he finally came upstairs.

'I thought you went with him to stop him going on the lawn,' I said.

'He began by walking round the rope very correctly. Then he must have got intoxicated by moonlight.'

'Or a cat,' I suggested.

'Quite,' agreed Charles. 'Anyway he was over the rope and through about ninety per cent of those cotton strands.'

From the bathroom Charles called to say that we must set the alarm clock for dawn. It wouldn't do to leave the grass seed to the birds, unprotected, for a number of light hours.

I don't think it was that year the lawn improved so much as the next when Richard went away to school, and we got a new roller lawnmower. At any rate it is now comparatively smooth and green, and the voice of Mr Bates is heard no more in the land.

Whenever I begin to garden I am oppressed by my ignorance. As in looking after a baby or learning a foreign language, two weeks of experience are worth months or even years with books of theory. The things I have done myself I know, but I have done so much less than I would like to have done. At this time of the year I realise that I am a beginner still. I am in the annual class, and that I well know is the kindergarten stage. However, I continue to be very fond of annuals while trying to build up a herbaceous border, which is one stage further on, for the inhabitants of a herbaceous border are largely perennials with annual stems, and I am successful enough with delphiniums, lupins, hollyhocks, and the grey-leaved opium poppies to feel that I will soon be able to try more ambitious experiments. Pansies, antirrhinums and wallflowers are perennials, but usually treated as annuals. I have, of course, discovered, rather through neglect than good management, that wallflowers will, if left, turn into large perfumed bushes, that pansies will often last successfully through the winter.

In March I find myself spending a long time over seed catalogues, and also poring over the brilliant displays of seed packets in shops. Again I am in the lowest section of the gardening community, for I still prefer seed packets with large bright flowers on them to the more austere, and of course usually superior, plain packets with something like 'Helleborus Niger' printed on them. Which reminds me that when I was reading about the Christmas rose in an old herbal recently (date about 1814), the writer put in a warning that if danger of poisoning was to be avoided the apothecary should cultivate the plant itself in his garden. In an even older flower book helleborus niger was described as loving pure air. 'The species does not thrive very near London.' This is discouraging, but on the other hand the helleborus niger is apt to lose its exquisite purity even when grown in very pure air, and far from London. It is a good plan, I find, to put a little straw under the leaves and flowers to keep them lifted from wet and muddy ground.

Yes, in March one can indulge in a dream of flowers. The disillusion, the failures are non-existent. Beds of annuals glow in your mind. This year you are going to grow more stocks, so that you can have masses of perfumed palest pink and heliotrope blossoms, delicately set off by grey-green leaves. Ten-week stocks for day and night-scented stocks for after sundown. You remember with gratitude that sweet william will grow almost anywhere, and resolve to try some of the dwarf varieties for borders.

They are like brilliant velvety pincushions. Then, too, there are the eschscholtzias, or Californian poppies, which are obtainable now in all imaginable shades of yellow, from burnt orange, to palest white-gold. These are easy to grow in masses, as are larkspurs, those enchanting miniature delphiniums. Once you have had these you are pretty sure to have them again, and the same applies to love-in-a-mist and cornflowers, and aquilegias—the last will grow in the shade. Clarkia delight me, and so do godetias, though both have ugly names—they are in the Chinese tradition, frail, crumpled and softly tinted, and these with candytuft and mallows pink and white can be grown in effective masses. There are two schools of thought about the thinning of annuals, but a happy medium seems to be what one must aim at, and certainly the best way to support annuals is to push bushy twigs among them early in their growth. This saves the cat-has-rolled-here appearance which is apt to afflict annuals often after a heavy rainstorm.

I don't think we have any modern equivalent of *The Botanical Magazine or Flower Garden Displayed*, which was printed in 1787. The first volume of this is dedicated to 'Mrs Montague Burgoyne ; not less esteemed for her social and domestic virtues than admired for the accuracy with which she draws and the delicacy with which she paints the Beauties of Flora.' Certainly Mrs Burgoyne could not have been responsible for the painting of the Carpatian bell-flower, for the page opposite that drawing says sternly, 'Our figure, from a deficiency in the colouring art, gives a very inadequate idea of its beauty.' But on the whole the hand-coloured steel engravings in this book are extremely beautiful, and looking through the pages is rather like looking at an array of beautiful ghosts. Where are the Franklin's tartan, a scarlet bizarre carnation, the prim hoop-petticoat narcissus, the purple rudbeckia (' its outer petals are long, purple, pendulous ') and the rosa muscosa (' where is the painter and poet who has not celebrated the beautiful moss rose ? ') ?

And now with the crocus vernus, enduring cheerfully as they do the most uninspiring conditions at the stony edge of a border. I found this eighteenth-century entry about the preservation of crocuses if not of practical value at least thought provoking :

' The most mischievous of all our common birds, the sparrow, is very apt to commit great depredation amongst crocuses when in flower, to the no small mortification of those who delight in their culture. We have succeeded in keeping these birds off by placing near the crocuses the skin of a cat properly stuffed.'

How does one stuff a cat, properly or improperly ?

I prefer to return to my contemplation of seeds, to the refrain which runs through one's head in March, ' I must have some miniature Michaelmas daises this year—Countess of Dudley, rose pink and another lavender, and I must have . . .'

READING FORGOTTEN BOOKS DURING SPRING CLEANING

Nobody can doubt that spring-cleaning has its bright moments. What delight I had, for instance, in an old copy of the *Family Friend*, 1880, in which the following answers to correspondents appear :

Ernest Goethe writes to ask whether we would be likely to accept a tale which has occupied his head and pen for two years, the title of which is, *The March of the Mad House, or Lost Ann of Lucerne.*

Whatever tales we print will have some immediate good purpose in view. If we may judge of the tale by its title, we would rather decline our correspondent's romance.

W-l-m, Churchill. We shall be glad to see your papers respecting 'Vulgar Antiquities.' They should be brief and lively.

A Lynn Correspondent. We have no space to devote to love epistles. H.J.C. may be a very dear creature, but you can find other modes of expressing your devotion than by poems through the *Family Friend.*

Meggie. We will do our best to provide a pattern for the much-desired night-cap.

Agnes. We cannot say who was the original inventor of Torser Work. If Miss Sharrar claims the invention, it is probably hers.

Declined with Thanks. 'Lines on Spring' by H.C.; 'Lines on the Use of Snuff'; 'The Moss Rose' by A.L.P.; 'A Chapter on Feline Characteristics'; 'The Wife's Secret.'

H.M.V. You *would* do wrong to ask a favour from the Queen. Apart from the propriety of your doing so, your chances of success are hopeless.

G.S. Take less animal food. Drink water, don't smoke, and order yourself to be pulled out of bed at a fixed hour, *without mercy*. In a few weeks you will learn to get up by yourself.

G.S. asks: Does infinite space admit of a centre—and if it does, where is it?

The centre—to us—is No. 8 St Peter's Terrace, Islington.

Alice. A lady is *not* an old maid at the age of twenty-four. A woman is in her prime between thirty-five and forty-five. Ill nature often assigns the term 'old maid' to unmarried females long before their best years have arrived. Alas, many young wives had better have remained old maids.

A.D. A letter addressed to the Carlton Club, London, will probably find the Count de Montemolin. We have not his private address.

M.T. Would it be proper to offer a gentleman in church, who is a stranger, half the book you are using?

Probably better than offering half the book would be to present it altogether, and to accept the partial use of it, if solicited by the offer of the stranger.

Declined with Thanks. ' The Seaweed's Lament ' ; ' A Snowdrop ' (good but not perfect) ; ' Grave Yard Thoughts.'

A Gentleman Subscriber says he would be greatly obliged if we would insert in this agreeable little miscellany a few sprinklings of experimental philosophy, and chemistry, as he can understand very little about knitted lace collars and the like.

Gallantry, please, Sir. Look upon the wrists and necks of your fair companions, and upon sofas, sideboards and pianos for neat productions of knitting and netting, and thank the *Family Friend*.

REALISING THE LOOSE COVERS HAVE HAD IT

How is it that the pieces of newspaper wrapping the fish show items of absorbing interest? I feel I must read them, because they seem so much more interesting than those in my own paper, and many is the paragraph I have avidly pursued through grey fish-smelling dampness or bloodstains. Between fish scales the other day I read 'New Loose Covers for 4d.' As I had been wearing rose-coloured glasses steadily for months every time I went into the sitting-room I read this with great attention, hoping to pick up some idea of how this miracle could be performed. The 4d, it turned out, was for stitching thread. The writer of the article said blithely that she carefully removed the backs of chair and settee covers and used the good pieces of linen thus obtained to cover the worn parts. All right. I could do that. But unless you live in a room where all the furniture has its back to a wall, an impossible situation I should have thought, what does one do about the backs? Do they remain shamelessly naked, or does one stitch in lengths of dyed sheeting or old curtains or arrange tasteful displays of family photographs in the gaps, or what? No, this fourpenny dream is not for me, I can see. On the other hand something will have to be done. The most successful covers I had during the time of coupons were made out of army paliasse covers. These are getting scarce now, but they were obtainable from Army and Navy stores, and were, the best of them, made of heavy natural linen. They were depressing to look at, being the shapes of large coffins, but, reduced to more inviting sizes they made wonderful covers. Now I dally with various ideas, petunia-linen covers, curtains of duck-egg blue, and white walls ; or alternatively pale-green walls, daffodil-yellow curtains and chocolate-brown covers. Maybe grey covers, white cushions, claret-coloured curtains and pelmets and white walls would be attractive. Or if I had a copy of eighteenth-century glazed chintz in fondant pink and grey, with a lime-green ceiling, and white walls. Delightful, I'd like to try all or any. The only difficulty in the way is the cost. Surely, looking at my shabby chair I can't possibly be regretting the good old days when it was natural-coloured linen or nothing, and my mind was made up for me ?

MARSHMALLOW TART

THIS is a good solid sweet to have following a light first supper course—say salad and cold meat. It looks rather extravagant, and of course isn't, and it can be made, except for the marshmallow top dressing, with other pastry earlier in the day, or even the day before, if you intend to warm it up for the actual meal.

Ingredients

½ lb. Self-raising flour	*¼ lb. Lard, or lard and margarine mixed*
Pinch of salt	
¼ lb. Marshmallows	*Sliced apples, or dried stewed apricots, or peaches, or plum jam*
A few chopped nuts	

The idea is to make an open fruit or jam tart, trellis it with twisted strips of pastry so that it is divided into squares, and bake. The layer of fruit or jam in the tart wants to be an ample one, and I recommend those fruits or jams with a slightly sharp flavour. Just before the meal cut marshmallows in two and place each half in a square of pastry trellising. Place the tart under the grill, and brown very lightly. Sprinkle with chopped nuts. If you want the tart to be hot it can wait in a cool oven while the first course is being eaten. If you want to be specially luxurious, coffee ice cream goes very well with this.

VISIT TO AN AUTOMATIC TELEPHONE EXCHANGE

TELEPHONES are like people and have definite characters of their own. The thing to aim at seems to be a placid telephone with a number which is not a temptation to careless diallers. Early numbers 1, 2, 3, in whatever mixture they follow each other, are easy to dial wrongly. Recently I went with children and a friend to look round the local telephone exchange—and it was made quite clear to us, not so much that it was easy for things to go wrong, as that it was miraculous that they nearly always went right. I believe, if you are interested, that it is always possible to arrange to look round the exchange, and certainly such a visit makes a most instructive excursion for yourself as well as children.

Our telephone, I should have said, off-hand, had had a quiet uneventful existence, but viewing its life history typed on the card : 'due to snow,' 'continuous sounding of bell,' etc., and once the shameful words 'disconnected—A/C unpaid,' I remembered all over again the feeling of frustration which came over me when I returned from six weeks' absence one summer to find the telephone dead.

In another part of the exchange you could see the figure at which your account stood at that moment—a little metal row of figures. In another the forest of intertwined red and green wires were looped and coiled together like magnificent tropical vines, and among them it was possible to see just where your own wire went.

Perhaps the most interesting department is that in which you can see the automatic system actually at work. You walk down long corridors with six to eight columns of grey canisters on either side of you; the air is full of clicks, and electric bulbs flash on and off. Here the strange process which starts when you dial a number is going on all round you. The member of the staff takes down a grey canister, which turns out to be half a canister, and goes away to dial a number, and you watch the machine in front of you find the number as he dials. ' Hunting up ' is the expressive phrase used. We stood hopefully in front of our number, but nobody was ringing us up at that moment; the telephone was silent in the empty house. We went away, very slowly, with backward glances, hoping for a miracle.

THE TIRED WOMAN'S EPITAPH

Quoted before 1850, and said to date from 1744, from Bushey, Hertfordshire

Here lies a poor woman, who always was tired ;
She lived in a house where help was not hired.
Her last words on earth were : ' Dear friends, I am going
Where washing ain't done, nor sweeping, nor sewing ;
But everything there is exact to my wishes ;
For where they don't eat there's no washing of dishes.
I'll be where loud anthems will always be ringing,
But, having no voice, I'll be clear of the singing.
Don't mourn for me now ; don't mourn for me never—
I'm going to do nothing for ever and ever.

ANON.

GRASMERE JOURNAL (1802)

(*March 27th*) *Saturday*. A divine morning. At breakfast William wrote part of an ode. Mr Olliff sent the dung and Wm. went to work in the garden. We sate all day in the orchard.

(*April 15th*) *Thursday*. When we were in the woods beyond Gowbarrow Park we saw a few daffodils close to the water-side. We fancied that the lake had floated the seeds ashore, and that the little colony had so sprung up. But as we went along there were more and yet more ; and at last, under the boughs of the trees, we saw that there was a long belt of them along the shore, about the breadth of a country turnpike road. I never saw daffodils so beautiful. They grew among the mossy stones about and about them ; some rested their heads upon these stones as on a pillow for weariness ; and the rest tossed and reeled and danced, and seemed as if they verily laughed with the wind, that blew upon them over the lake ; they looked so gay, ever glancing, ever changing. . . .

DOROTHY WORDSWORTH

'I WANDERED LONELY AS A CLOUD'

(Grasmere 1804)

I WANDERED lonely as a cloud
That floats on high o'er vales and hills,
When all at once I saw a crowd,
A host, of golden daffodils ;
Beside the lake, beneath the trees,
Fluttering and dancing in the breeze.

Continuous as the stars that shine
And twinkle on the milky way,
They stretched in never-ending line
Along the margin of a bay :
Ten thousand saw I at a glance,
Tossing their heads in sprightly dance.

The waves beside them danced ; but they
Out-did the sparkling waves in glee :
A poet could not but be gay,
In such a jocund company :
I gazed—and gazed—but little thought
What wealth the show to me had brought :

For oft, when on my couch I lie
In vacant or in pensive mood,
They flash upon that inward eye
Which is the bliss of solitude ;
And then my heart with pleasure fills,
And dances with the daffodils.

WILLIAM WORDSWORTH

APRIL

April. *This Month sow Hemp, and Flax, Pole Hops, set and sow all kinds of Garden Herbs. Restore the liberty of the laborious Bee by opening her Hive. Bark Trees for Tanners ; and let good Huswives mind their gardens and begin to think of their Daries.*

In Gardening never this rule forget
To sow dry, and set wet.

Use of Physick becomes now seasonable ; as also Purging and Blood-letting. It is good to abstain from Wine ; or many Diseases will be taken thereby to the ruin of Many.

This Month the Pores of the Body are open, and apt to receive Physick ; therefore this is the best time to remove causes of sickness, or for speedy remedy in extremities, Pray to God for Blessing. **British Merlin, 1677**

THE BUCKET ON THE LADDER

I KNOW a woman who when she spoke of spring cleaning meant redecorating. I've heard of another who was so rich (before the war) that when she was tired of her flat she used to ring up a firm of interior decorators, go to a hotel to live, and not move back until the transformation was complete. These wholesale conceptions of the annual attempt to be, if not godly, next to it, are not mine. Mine is much more ordinary, and much worse. It is a mixture of redecorating and trying to persuade yourself that this room will go for another year, without redecorating, and making pots of tea for workmen, looking at curtain material, washing paint, and wondering how some women seem to have hands which show no marks of toil, although you know that if there is one flower they are not like, it is the lily of the field.

I have known times during spring cleaning when I felt an alien in my own house. This most often happens when the kitchen is being redecorated. I remember one period when we decided that the removal of one piece of wall in our kitchen, and the installation of a new sink would make all the difference. So it did. The workmen arrived, and though the personnel shifted a little from time to time, they came to stay. I forgot what it was like to go into a kitchen and cook a meal without having to walk a gangplank to get water.

'Drink their heads off they will,' said Mrs Cartwright gloomily on the first day. 'They like their tea as black as a thunderstorm.'

Most of the kitchen furniture was put out in the garden with tarpaulins over it. The rest made going through the passage to the kitchen a sort of obstacle race. The water was turned off, and a sort of savage hammering went on for hour after hour.

Then the dust descended on us. The removal of one wall released the dust of ages, and nothing would keep it out of the rest of the house.

'We might as well get on with the spring cleaning of the sitting-room,' I said to Mrs Cartwright, idly writing my name in the dust on the top of a bookshelf. 'We can't make things worse.'

'That's where I think you're wrong, Mum,' said Mrs Cartwright. 'Where's the curtains and covers to be washed with the water off? And the sweep's not been told.'

That last point was too much for me. Telling the sweep is the ground plan of spring cleaning. Until he has been told, and has come—either in a white van painted on the side with 'Electric Sweep: Why Muddle along with the old when you can Sweep Clean with the new?'; or on a bike with a sack on the handle-bars—there is little you can do.

'I might as well put the kettle on the nursery gas ring for a cup of tea,' says Mrs Cartwright. 'It's just a case of stick it.'

By this time workmen were cheerfully walking down the garden path wheeling barrows full of rubble.

'They seem to be getting on quite fast,' I said hopefully, pleased that the hammering had accomplished something.

'It's all right while they're breaking things up,' said Mrs Cartwright. 'You just wait till they start making something. It's my belief that they wouldn't draw a breath if it wasn't for dying if they don't. You wait till they start putting them tiles in.'

New tiles were being put in round the sink, and on the

floor round the sink, and I had to agree that Mrs Cartwright was right.

'It's not a job you can hurry,' said the tiler, stirring his tea vigorously. 'I knew one chap who put on a turn of speed, didn't set the tiles in regular, and left a corner sticking up sixteenth of an inch. You wouldn't think that 'ud matter, would you?'

'But it did, of course,' I said, taking the safe line.

'Yes, the lady fell flat on her face, and broke her nose. She never looked quite the same after that.'

I went away and left him shaking his head. It was better on the whole, I felt, to leave him to his own speed.

'They won't be finished by the week-end,' said Charles, eating toast in the nursery.

'But they've been here two days already!' I said. 'They can't take three more!'

'Can't they!' said Charles.

On Friday afternoon the boss came round with pay packets, and the cigarette smoke in the kitchen became even more dense.

'Aren't you coming in tomorrow morning to clear up?' I asked.

The man who was fixing up a sort of Emmet bridge over the cement to the sink shook his head, while another swept up, raising a fresh cloud of dust, and a third collected tools.

'It ain't worth it, Mam,' he said. 'I can get in a bit of rabbit shooting out in the country in the morning, and I don't have to pay tax on that. No, you'll have a nice week-end free of us, you'll be glad I reckon. Sorry you can't have no hot water.'

'On Monday we start on scraping the walls,' said the man who was sweeping the floor. 'Two coats, if not three, these walls want. Shocking they are.'

I looked defensively, but helplessly, on walls which had seemed moderately clean and whole a week ago, but now with no sheltering furniture looked scarred and faded.

I tottered up and down the Emmet plank all the week-end, and on Monday the gang in the kitchen were reinforced by two decorators, and a boy to sweep up and take away the stuff they scraped off.

'Is this the blue you had in mind, madam?' asked the senior decorator.

'It looks a bit dark doesn't it?' I said, peering into navy blue depths. I had planned a blue-and-white kitchen —white from shoulder height, and had given the blue of a striped Cornish pottery jar as a pattern for the blue paint.

'That's the blue you said. It's the way the light falls,' he said very firmly.

I feel that where dealing with decorators is concerned there are two methods. One is to insist on having what you want, and the other is to have what they've got. In theory I belong to the first group. In practice I more often than not fall into the second. Worn down by their occupation of the house, and the feeling that if I have something different they will be there much longer, I accept what they want, suppressing the thought of all the weeks and months ahead when I will be sorry for it.

'I'll try a bit round the gas stove,' he said. 'Then you can see.'

It still looked very dark to me.

'I mixed it specially for you,' he said. 'This colour isn't asked for in the general run of things. Blue's a hard shade to deal with.'

'It is darker than I thought it would be,' I said.

'Well, we'll leave it while the upper white's being done,' he said cheerfully. 'Perhaps I might lighten it a bit for you, but I can't guarantee any improvement. Might make it mauvish.'

'Oh, no!' I said. 'I couldn't bear mauve.'

'That's what I say. Now I like this colour myself. A good wearing shade. But on the other hand it's you who've got to live with it.'

I agreed that it was, but was too battered to do more about it at the moment.

'It'll grow on you!' he told me as we parted.

I don't know what made him relent. As far as I was concerned we were going to have the dark-blue paint, but the next morning he arrived with another can which I could see at once was practically the shade I wanted.

'I found meself thinking about the blue in bed last night,' he said. 'And I thought, she doesn't really like the dark blue.'

'Well, I do feel it's a little dark,' I said.

'I guessed you did,' he said triumphantly.

The beautiful climax in the kitchen came when, the tiles having set, and the sink having been installed, only two decorators, a plumber and a carpenter were still at work. The gas man arrived to put back the thermostatic heater over the sink. I heard a splintering crash.

'It's all right,' said Mrs Cartwright, coming over and looking pleased and tragic all at once. 'That's about put the tin lid on it. The gas man's been and sat through the window.'

'How?' I asked, being unable to visualise it.

'He bent down sharp to look at the boiler, and his back'—Mrs Cartwright paused delicately—'went through the window side of the sink there.'

'I hope he isn't hurt!' I said.

'Hurt!' Mrs Cartwright laughed. 'He's not hurt! It's the window wot's hurt.'

I suppose most people learned to do some house decoration during and after the war, and having learnt prefer to go on. It was a case then of doing it yourself or not having it done at all.

I remember with gratitude an ex-naval man of fifty-five or so who came to do some decorating for me in the time he could spare away from his own job. He was an expert painter and distemperer, but could not spare time to do all that needed doing to our house. I had returned with the children after being away for four years, and in a matter of months expected Charles home from India. Mr Baines didn't hold with women doing ceilings. He thought they weren't built for it. He offered, moreover, to do the ceilings, and while he was engaged on the long job of redecorating the main rooms downstairs, which I felt I couldn't tackle, he would keep an eye on what I did in more obscure places. From him I learnt the elementary but indispensable things: to mix distemper with warm water and to mix it very thoroughly; to vary shades with red and yellow ochre; to keep distemper and paint brushes in clean water when not in use; never to skimp the preliminary work of scraping, and filling holes with plaster; to keep two brushes of varying thickness in hand while painting. At the end of a fortnight or so I had progressed so well that Mr Baines even offered to lend me one or two of his brushes; this I regarded as a great compliment. He assured me that a bad painter could ruin a brush in ten minutes. I don't know if this is an accurate statement or not, but I know that there is a sort of rhythm of movement that you catch after you have been painting for a time which you know instinctively is the right one. Without this, clumsy work with an overloaded brush is inevitable.

While we painted Mr Baines entertained me with many stirring tales of the sea. One in particular I liked about the time when the warship on which he was serving was anchored in a Spanish bay. Apparently the rubbish from the galleys sent through the shutes into the sea was regarded by the local fishermen as far too valuable for fishes, and they used to congregate with their nets at the end of the shute and collect, often with shouts of glee, what came down. There was one enormous Spaniard who used to sit, with a knife gleaming on the seat beside him, directly under the shute, and make it impossible for other fishermen to get pickings. After a time this struck the crew as grossly unfair, and they decided to stop it.

'We got some firebricks from the stokers,' said Mr Baines with satisfaction, 'and sent those down the shute. Talk about the air being blue! The firebricks went straight through the net, of course, cut it up nicely. The fellow rowed off cursing and waving his knife at us. Still, it meant the others had a chance. Fair's fair, even with rubbish.'

It was Mr Baines's tuition that made me feel brave enough to tackle the worst job—and that was to strip the papers off one of the nicest bedrooms in the house—a very big attic room of charming shape which had once been used as a day nursery. I wanted this for a guest room, and it seemed to me that the time had come to stop compromising—that is, distempering over what was underneath. There was so much underneath I despaired of ever coming to an end. There were at least three layers of paper, a Victorian trellis of red roses and blue ribbons, a spring symphony of violets, daffodils and love birds, and finally something Edwardian and full blown, tea-roses I think.

Luckily, as the room was out of the general traffic of the house I could do the job slowly. Damping and scraping took a very long time indeed, and when it was finally done and the last soggy bucket had been emptied into the dustbin, I was appalled at the roughness of the walls. I could see why they had been papered, but I dared not tackle paper myself. I knew the result would resemble that achieved by the Marx brothers in *A Day at the Races*. Therefore it had to be distemper. Filling the holes was another long job, but at last the surface was more or less even. Then I was faced with the prospect of putting on two coats of distemper, and in some sections of the room, where the Victorian builders seemed to have applied a substance which looked like tar to the walls, three. I had decided on a colour scheme of palest pink, that is white tinged with pink, and oyster grey paint. Of course both these shades were unobtainable and had to be mixed specially. A very little pink added to ivory gave me the warm tone I wanted. I used flat French grey paint as an undercoat on the woodwork, and this in contrast to the walls looked hyacinth blue. Obviously the top coat had to be quite different. Finally pink in tiny quantities was added to a mushroom grey. The result was warm and light, and gave what I wanted, a cheerful effect to the darkest part of the room where the eaves came down. Pink is difficult to work with because it is so easy to get it too dark, and nothing is more horrible than a too-pink room. Remember that distemper dries a couple of shades lighter, but if you use pink be very sparing indeed with it. A white distemper should always have a little pink added to it.

The housing shortage has made people ingenious, and some of the most delightful results have been obtained when people of taste have dealt with houses that from an artistic point of view looked utterly hopeless. Not long ago I was taken to see a house in the working-class district of a small coast town. The street was long and dull, the houses of the small narrow-fronted type which were built towards the end of the last century. They were all joined together except for narrow tunnel passages between every second house. A lady, the widow of an artist, took one of these houses. It literally was the only one she could get, and she transformed it.

The door from the street had opened straight into the front sitting-room. A narrow staircase separated this room from the back room. A small lobby separated the back room from a tiny scullery. None of the windows would open, the doors would hardly close and the handles were old brass knobs which rattled palsiedly. Every room had an old brown dirty paper ; in one of the three bedrooms upstairs the floor was so rotten that the bed legs were imbedded in it. The fireplaces were black and of the high Victorian basket shape. The house was wired for electricity, but the electric meter was planted on the wall of the sitting-room with the wiring exposed. In the tiny scullery was a crooked shallow sink, an old rusty fireplace and a cement boiler. Outside there was an old-fashioned lavatory and coal-shed closed in with mouldering doors and a galvanised fence set in a cement floor. The garden itself was a tumble of weeds, ashes and old tins.

There could not possibly have been less promising material.

Yet when I saw it the new owner, who is French, had made it into a charming little house, full of light and air, and with a pretty vista of rooms following each other from the front to the back so that an illusion of space was given.

In the front sitting-room she put leaded glass into the

upper third of the front door, which immediately offset the effect of the too-small window. She had the old fireplace removed and the aperture blocked flat with the wall, put a few neutral tiles on the floor and installed an electric fire. The whole room including the two cupboards on either side of the fireplace was painted and distempered a light ivory. Block handles were put on the doors. The narrow staircase was stripped and distempered and painted ivory, too, as was the back room. From this the old fireplace was removed, and a slow combustion stove with surrounding light neutral tiles installed. The electric meter was put under the stairs! The tiny lobby between the back room and the old scullery was left because the back door opened into it, and when I saw it I thought it added greatly to the illusion of space. The black range and boiler were removed from the scullery, and the end wall half removed to put in a door. This door eventually led to the bathroom, contrived out of the space which had been occupied by the outside lavatory and tool- and coal-shed. The kitchen floor had been removed and cemented, and a rubber composition floor put down. An electric cooker, a gas water-heater over the deep sink under the window, and a small gas refrigerator made the small kitchen convenient. There was just room in the ex-tool-shed for a built-in bath and a washbasin, and a gas thermostatic water-heater with a swivel tap which served both bath and basin. An electric heater was set high on the wall. From the bathroom another door led to the lavatory.

Outside the galvanised iron fence was painted light cream, so that reflected light from it came into the kitchen, bathroom and back room, and a little cement was broken at the base so that a row of plants and trellis could be placed there. A small tool-shed and coal-house was built on to the end wall of the lavatory, and all the outside paintwork was ivory (bricks ivory washed) and pale green. The rubbish was cleared from the garden, a lawn laid, set round with lavender and thyme bushes. Two tiny cypress trees added to the charmingly prim and orderly effect.

Inside all the windows were curtained with pale-écru net, and pelmets of hardboard painted ivory had been added in each case to hide curtain hooks and rails. The carpeting was fitted felt in pale shades. Add in your mind lamps and pictures and a few pieces of old china, candlewick covers in the bedrooms, comfortable, but not too large chairs, a miraculously achieved air of space and light, and you can see how a Victorian monstrosity was turned into a house of character and charm.

PUTTING UP A NEW PICTURE

ONE of the pleasant things about spring cleaning is changing the pictures round after it is all over, or better still hanging a new one for the first time. It is always delightful to buy a picture, especially an original by an artist one knows, and to see how it gives new life to a room. Changing the pictures round is very nearly as good as buying a new one. Our house, with its narrow hall, is greatly lightened by having the front door open, and as the house is set well back from the road it usually is open. I've been interested to see how tradesmen waiting on the step have reacted to the pictures in the hall. There was one laundry man who was so fascinated by a reproduction of Paul Nash's *South Downs* that he came into the hall each Monday to look at it. 'I've never seen trees like that,' he said, 'but it gets you.' When it was changed for an engraving of Wadham College, Oxford, he expressed his entire disapproval. An original-pen-and ink drawing of the tumble of roofs behind our town hall was the choice of the baker's roundsman, who said that was his idea of what a picture should be. When I suggested that he should save up and buy a similar one for the artist lived in the town, he seemed both embarrassed and elated by the idea.

Roddy and I had an enjoyable post-spring cleaning evening when we *passe-partout* half a dozen Victorian fashion plates for the guest room. They had been given to me by a friend who had grouped a dozen or so of them most effectively on the white pin-spot paper of her dining-room. The pretty simpering faces and fabulous dresses of 1830 made a series of charming little pictures. 'The Isabeau paletot is half-fitting. It is made of light maroon cloth, and richly trimmed with two rows of *passementerie*. . . . For the evening a white muslin demi-toilette over a muslin slip is the most appropriate. It is trimmed with splendid roses from the darkest purple to the delicate pink of the malmaison. . . . A charming toilette of Havannah garland in serpent blue. . . . A bonnet of mauve taffetas trimmed with Neapolitan violets.'

The Most Disliked Job of the Month—April

O.H.£M.S.

I HAVE never been able to understand why the income-tax year should end in April. It seems the wrong time for any consideration of finance. I suppose realists would say there is little truth in the statement that the best things in life are free, but that lambs turn into mutton, and blossoms into expensive apples and pears, and so the spring is the best time to consider your budget. Lavish display of any kind means expense for somebody, they would gloomily point out. Of all ways of earning a living authorship is among the worst when it comes to income tax. Accuracy and self-control are called for in large measure. Accuracy to make a correct return, and self-control to save half of what you earn to pay the income tax.

In America, I hear, it is much worse. The income-tax forms there contain instructions like these :

'If line 6 is over 400 dollars but not over 100,000 dollars enter 52 plus 9 per cent of the excess over 400 dollars.'

For eleven months it has been evident that you earn far far too little, but in April, the Chaucerian golden month, when money ought to have less importance than buttercups, it is clear that you earned far too much, and that all, all of it, has mysteriously gone.

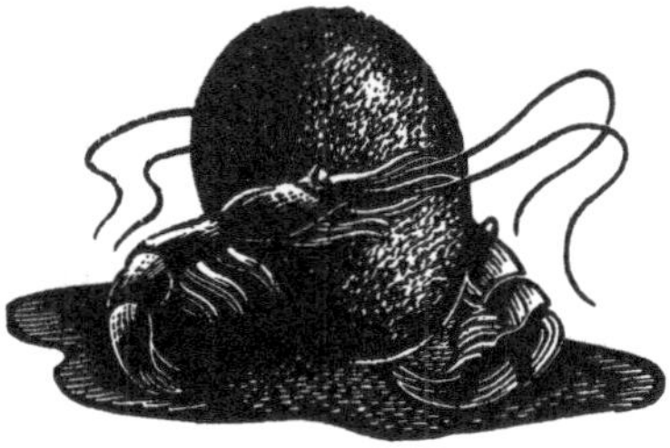

EGGS AND SHRIMPS (GRAND)

HERE are two ways of combining eggs and shrimps for supper dishes in a long light April evening. The first looks beautiful, the second looks less so, but tastes just as good. Don't be put off by the bother of making a ring mould. It is worth the slight extra trouble because it makes it so easy to arrange your salad. You can make tomato aspic simply by using a good tomato soup or seasoned juice as liquid for your aspic jelly.

Ingredients

- 8 *to* 9 *in. Ring mould of tomato aspic*
- 1½ *cups Shrimps (bottled, tinned or fresh)*
- 1 *cup Thinly chopped celery*
- ½ *cup Walnuts*
- ¼ *cup Olives*
- ½ *cup Mayonnaise (your own or bottled)*
- 1 *or* 2 *Hard-boiled eggs (optional)*
- *Sliced tomatoes*

Method

Make the tomato aspic one day ahead, or in the morning for supper. Shortly before serving blend the shrimps, celery, walnuts, olives with mayonnaise. Fill centre of mould with mixture, and decorate with shrimps, sliced tomato and eggs.

EGGS AND SHRIMPS (*plain and hot*)

Ingredients

2 *Hard-boiled eggs*
½ *pint Milk*
½ *oz. Flour*
1½ *cup Shrimps*
1 *oz. Margarine*
1 *tablespoonful Grated cheese*
Seasoning

Method

Put shrimps in a greased fireproof dish. Slice eggs and put on top of shrimps. Melt margarine in saucepan, add flour, mix well, add milk, pepper and salt and a little of the cheese ; stir well, let it boil for a minute or two, add chopped parsley, and then pour over eggs and shrimps. Sprinkle the rest of the cheese over the top, and brown in a hot oven.

VISIT TO A NURSERY GARDEN

I CAN'T remember a time when we didn't enjoy visiting a nursery garden in April. There is something attractive about every part of a nursery, from the large sweet-smelling hothouses where hyacinths are still standing in pots for sale, to the rain-water tanks, and the dark sheds with glowing red eyes set in them where the stoking is done.

Buying plants from a shop is dull compared with choosing them yourself from a nursery. To walk down a cindery path between rows of polyanthus, surely more treacley-brown, cinnamon-brown, buttery-yellow, creamy-yellow than polyanthus anywhere else, is a good curtain raiser. So pleasant to stop every now and again and say, ' What's that ? Couldn't we grow that ? ' Then comes the search for the nurseryman himself. One always hopes he will not be found too soon, for while you are looking you can get a glimpse of corners you might otherwise have missed.

Summer comes rushing at you as you pass an open greenhouse door, not because of the colour, for inside are to be seen merely rank upon rank of tiny geraniums—most likely part of the summer bedding plants for the park—but because of all smells that of rain on warm damp earth is one of the best.

Beyond a pile of coke you see groups of pointed brilliantly red leaves beyond glass, and remember one of the children in a book by Enid Bagnold who refers to ' meaty red plants.'

In another greenhouse wait the potted chrysanthemums, which were divided in December and January, and will be planted out next month. In another tomatoes spread lacy leaves to the warmth, and you remember you must order some.

Perhaps the nurseryman is found near the bedding plants which are actually ready for sale now. Pansies, purple-black, yellow, chocolate-streaked or brindled cream and brown, turn their soft inquiring faces up at you. There are button daisies, reminiscent of clean pink-and-white cotton dresses and nicely brushed hair ; and dark, red-veined antirrhinums ; or petunias with greyish hairy leaves. There are stocks here, too, and tobacco flowers.

' A bit soon for bedding out,' he says, ' but I'll send you what you want when I think it's time.'

' I don't see any nemesia,' I say.

The nursery man looks patient.

' I was hoping you weren't doing to say that. Every lady who has come in today has asked for nemesia. And why ? Because they did well last year. Doesn't follow they will this year. More than likely they won't. But it's always like that. Petunias good one year, and next year nobody wants anything but petunias.'

But we end up amicably in the ordering shed, where he puts down 6 doz. pet., 4 doz. nem., 2 doz. nic., 6 doz. ant., 3 doz. toms., in a large earthy book.

Perhaps we ask if he has any tulips left over, and he says he has been too busy to pick any today, but if we like we can pick what we want and go and show him the bunch and he'll say how much it is. And we know it won't be anything like as much as we'd pay for them in the shops. 'Always cut out the middleman,' he shouts cheerfully after us.

Cutting out the middleman when it is a question of picking tulips is one thing, I think, but going to the pit head, for instance, and fetching your own coal is quite another.

COLD COMFORT FARM

FLORA approached the hut in some trepidation. Her practical experience of confinements was non-existent, for such of her friends as were married had not yet any children, and most of them were still too young to think of marriage as anything but a state infinitely remote.

But she had a lively acquaintance with confinements through the works of women novelists, especially those of the unmarried ones. Their descriptions of what was coming to their less fortunate married sisters usually ran to four or five pages of close print, or eight or nine pages of staccato lines containing seven words, and a great many dots arranged in threes.

Another school dismissed confinements with a careful brightness, a 'so-sorry-I'm-late-darling-I've-just-been-having-a-baby-where-shall-we-go-for-supper-afterwards ?' sang-froid which Flora, curiously enough, found equally alarming.

She sometimes wondered whether the old-fashioned, though doubtless lazy, method of describing the event in the phrase, 'She was brought to bed of a fine boy,' was not the best way of putting it.

A third type of woman novelist combined literature and motherhood by writing a good, serious first novel when they were twenty-six ; then marrying and having a baby, and, the confinement over, writing articles for the Press on '"How I shall Bring Up My Daughter," by Miss Gwenyth Bludgeon, the brilliant young novelist, who gave birth to a daughter this morning. Miss Bludgeon is in private life Mrs Neil McIntosh.'

Some of Flora's friends had been exceedingly frightened, not to say revolted, by these painstaking descriptions of confinements ; and had been compelled to rush off to the Zoo and bribe the keepers to assure them that the lionesses, at least, got through the greatest event of their Lives in decent solitude. It was comforting, too, to watch the lionesses cuffing their fubsy cubs about in the sunlight. The lionesses, at least, did not write articles for the papers on how they would bring up their cubs.

STELLA GIBBONS

ANNALS OF MY VILLAGE

WHEN about to be occupied in maternal duties, the female rabbit relinquishes all her wonted habits, the wild companionship of her associates, the delights of the forest and the wild. This active creature submits to confinement, at the very moment when everything invites her abroad, and is for many days together fixed in her dark burrow, as closely as if her limbs were tied down by pins and wires. In order to render this burrow the more comfortable for her young, she makes a bed of the softest fur from her own warm garment, and never ventures out for the first two or three days . . . Thus secluded, she continues to cherish them for more than six weeks, during which the father never intrudes. At length the happy era of their deliverance approaches. The cautious parent timidly leads them to the entrance of the dormitory, where they nibble groundsel and other tender herbs, and the father seems to acknowledge them as his own. He takes them between his paws, smooths their soft hair, and licks them ; each in their turn equally partakes of his care and attention.

By the author of
The Select Female Biographer, 1814

ANGELICO GOLD

After the rain laburnums
Are loaded with yellow snow,
And buttercup fields are painted
With gold of Angelico.

Who never was in England
Yet magically could shew
The green and gold of English fields
On the walls of San Marco ;

And when he painted heaven
Would have his angels blow
Trumpets of gold on English lawns
Rain-washed an hour ago.

R. N. CURREY

May

May. *This Month command the provident Huswife and the prudent Artist to set their Stills on work. In the beginning of the Month sow and set those tender Summer Herbs that would not endure the formet cold. Weed your Hop Gardens, cut off superfluous Branches. Moss Trees and Gardens, and weed Corn; rise early, and walk the Fields and Gardens.*

Now every Garden and Hedge affords the Food and Physick. Rise early, walk the Fields by running streams the North and West Sides. Sage and Sweet Butter an excellent breakfast. Clarified Whay with Sage. Scurvy-Grass Ale and Wormwood Beer are wholesome Drinks. Green Whay excellent against Choler. Eat and drink betimes in the morning. Abstain from Meats that are hot in Nature and salt in quality.

British *Merlin*, 1677

Once, in a year which is unnamed in the notebook in which I kept it, but which must have been one in which flowers were plentiful, I kept a flower diary, putting down under each month the flowers which came and went in the house. I think it must have been before I had children, and life was more leisurely.

But flowers, leisure or not, money or not, are one of the greatest pleasures in life. There is no end to the interest one feels in the ideas which other women may give you about their arrangement. With this in mind I am putting down the entries in my flower diary in case some of the arrangements I found successful may be new to you.

I once knew a woman, an excellent housekeeper, far better than I can ever hope to be, who did not have flowers in her home because they added so considerably to the housework. She never had to pick up a rain of lupin flowers, or clean yellow pollen off a mantelshelf. She never had to think when a guest was coming of how among all the other jobs she could get a little bouquet to put on the dressing-table. She had never been pleased to buy three old bits of mirror and fit them into a bracket for a dark corner in a hall, so that a tiny bowl of flowers placed there could be reflected into a great jewel-like bunch. On the other hand, of course, she had never, as I have often done, made up for deficiencies in a room by eye-taking flowers.

During the years I have found that it is a good thing to try and keep one's flower vases uniform in colour and texture. I have a number of green glass bowls and jugs, and an equal number of pottery troughs and vases, and a few precious old pieces of china and pewter. I have no black bowls or jugs, and I'm sorry about this, as they make a splendid base for many flower arrangements. Off-white pottery is particularly valuable too. I think expensive cut glass often disappointing in design, and it takes all your ingenuity to make flowers look well in vases which, however sparkling, will not allow the flowers to spread naturally. Collecting good flower containers is a fascinating pursuit, and your greatest treasures are apt to arrive by accident. An old silver soup tureen, one of the kind which allows the domed top to swivel back under the rounded base, is an ideal container for June roses, and a massive china soup tureen, of the kind used in Victorian families, particularly if it is blue-and-white china, makes a most attractive home for a mixed display of bulbs. Old copper kettles, heavy old mugs of the type which used to be brought as presents from the seaside, or the gigantic sugar basins of sixty to seventy years ago, and some of the pieces from old china dressing-table sets, are other things you can use with success. China and glass rings are very pretty for tiny flowers, and particularly good for table decoration. Lighted candles and flowers go very well together. So next time you want to make a particularly charming display for a meal, try wedging candles at regular intervals in a flower ring. Once I bought a little basket filled with primroses from a gipsy, and this rough little container has been used over and over again for flowers which ask for informal arrangement. The big urn-shaped vases and tazzas, although lovely, are not so useful in the small house. If you have a number of plants in pots, cyclamen, primulas, and so on, and wish to group them, a big old china wash bowl tilted slightly forward with small plants at the front and tall ones at the back gives a very good effect.

It is always a good idea when you visit woods or the

seashore to collect any pebbles or stones which please you. These are invaluable. Not only can they be used with water for growing bulbs in glass troughs or bowls—crocuses, narcissi and hyacinths respond very happily to this method —but they hide holders which are usually unsightly. Irises, for instance, look very well if they are cut a little short and with their natural foliage arranged in a glass holder in a big flat bowl. Stones piled round the holder add greatly to the decorative effect, and the irises look as if they are actually growing.

Other things which I find make flower-arranging much easier are, of course, the usual crumpled pieces of wire netting ; or a strip of pliable lead about an inch wide which can be squeezed into different shapes inside a bowl ; a reel of rigid wire, and another of pin wire ; and a few pin-holders which cannot always be obtained but are worth looking for. The judicious use of wire takes you out of the amateur class of flower arrangers. Think what you could do with a piece of rigid wire curved into a hoop over a bowl of nasturtiums. The long trailing stems can be used most decoratively.

If you have a vase which is apt to dwarf flowers which perhaps have had their stems cut too short, you can put sand or crumpled tissue paper in the bottom of the vase to give added height to the flowers. Sand is excellent, too, to use for the arrangement of small flowers—crocuses, violets, pansies and scillas. Sand, or if you can't get sand, earth, in a bowl, with about a quarter of an inch of water over it, makes a good foundation for a little garden-in-the-house.

There are some flowers which are notably awkward for the house, although their colour in the garden makes you want to bring them in. Sweet Williams are velvety and beautiful, and yet they are clod-hopperish in the house.

They do not look well from below. Mixed with other flowers, and arranged almost horizontally, so that you look right at the crimson or salmon pink cushion of florets, they are at their best ; or they can look very well in a low bowl set in the niche of glass I mentioned earlier. Hydrangeas are too big and heavy except as a focal point of colour in some mixed arrangement; they look lovely in a long low container with sweet peas, or as part of a one-bloom line design—say, one hydrangea set in a low bowl with a ranged-out formal arrangement of foliage to offset it. The top florets of gladioli also make good line designs combined with their own foliage in low bowls. Here the pebbles come into use again. Poppies are so exquisitely coloured that one wants to have them in the house, and that is possible if they are picked when the first morsel of colour is breaking through the green calyx. Pick eschscholtzias and morning glories also in bud, and they will last well. Remember that blue, although one of the most glorious garden colours, badly needs sun, and is apt to be dull in the house.

I am always wanting to be more experimental than I am in this matter of growing bulbs and plants for the house. I have grown bulbs in water with pebbles, and try to get away from the conventional bowl of hyacinths or tulips. I've learnt that crocuses should be packed quite tightly in the earth or fibre, and when brought out of the dark at the end of eight weeks a little grass seed scattered on the top adds greatly to their decorative effect. One of the nicest bowls of bulbs I ever had gave me flowers for about two months. I placed close together crocuses, snowdrops, scillas, and a few daffodils and hyacinths in a big round yellow casserole, and, when the bulbs were coming up well, covered the top with moss. I've never actually tried to grow annuals in pots, but some of my friends who have greenhouses tell me they are most successful. If you have a cold frame they can, of course, be kept there till the approach of frost and then brought into the house. The seeds should be sown in August to come into bloom in the spring. The annual chrysanthemums, mignonette, spring-flowering stocks, nemesia and clarkia are all suitable.

Everybody has her favourite method of reviving drooping flowers. I have tried castor sugar with success. A penny at the bottom of a bowl of drooping tulips, and an aspirin, have both been known to work. I still think the quickest tonic when flowers are very limp after a long journey is to dip the stems in almost boiling water, but they will last longer, of course, if they can stand plunged up to their necks in a bucket of rainwater in a cool place for several hours, preferably overnight.

Branches of trees, lilac, pear, laburnum and hawthorn, should have the bark below the water-line peeled off, and all woody stems should be bruised at the end.

Beech leaves will keep most of the winter if crude glycerine is mixed with the water in which they are placed. It is also possible to preserve branches by placing them flat under a bedroom carpet covered with thick sheets of paper.

Here to end with is my flower diary :

January

Trails of young ivy and Christmas roses in a low bowl for a dinner table.

Cyclamen in pots.

A low bowl arranged with stones hiding the holders for the first bunches of snowdrops. A few twigs from an early budding sycamore hedge added.

A bowl of primroses dug up from the garden.

February

Branches of chestnut and beech in big earthenware jug forced in a sunny window.

A bowl of daffodils and forsythia—the daffodils arranged loosely.

A bowl of purple and white crocuses.

Anemones in a flower ring for the dinner table, and in an old green pottery jug for bedroom mantelpiece.

March

Big purple bowl of daffodils, pussy willow and branches of lime, for sitting-room.

Pewter jug of forsythia and narcissus.

A little field of daisies, celandines and violets arranged in big cream pottery bowl in hall.

Polyanthus dug up from garden in brown earthenware crock : they will be put back again when they stop flowering.

Two branches of japonica in a big flat bowl for lunch table.

April

A flowing design in a basket of daffodils, budding branches, narcissus, forsythia, and, as a focal point in bottom middle, grape hyacinths and polyanthus. This took a long time to arrange, but was worth it. The movement went from left to right, with the top left branches and flowers almost horizontal in a basket containing a tin of water, the smaller flowers bottom right cut short and also almost horizontal, the grape hyacinths and polyanthus facing front over basket edge.

Red tulips with cherry blossom in pewter in hall.

A flat bowl of horse-chestnut flowers.

A Victorian posy of little spring flowers, for bedroom.

Wallflowers, dark red, and grape hyacinths in an earthenware bowl.
A ring of grape hyacinths, primroses and polyanthus for dining-table.

May

Bluebell heads in a shallow bowl ringed with dark-red wallflowers.
Yellow tulips alone in green glass bowl.
Blue and-white-iris with red and white campion.
Double-white narcissus and pale-pink stocks in mauve-and-white Wedgewood jug.
White broom and pink tulips.
Deep-purple lilac in a pewter jug, its heaviness offset by pink and mauve tulips.
Heads of violas floating in a long copper tray.

June

A very misty and delicate arrangement of pinks, snapdragons, love-in-a-mist and pale-pink stocks.
Scabious spraying out from a centre of white sweet williams and salmon-pink sweet peas.
Old rose and chalk-pink stocks in a big crystal jug.
Pale-pink sweet peas and dianthus in a purple bowl.
A shallow basket filled with sprays of rambler.
White lilies and white lupins in a white pottery trough against a white wall. Lovely effect of shadows.
Pink peonies, clove pinks, dark-red sweet williams arranged with spraying-out purple loosestrife and foxgloves.
A big cottage-garden arrangement of sweet williams, roses, lupins, larkspur and marigolds.
Marigolds and purple pansies set between mirrors.

July

A silver bowl of lavender spikes, pink roses, picotees and gypsophila.

Sweet peas, mauve, and salmon-pink, spiked with lavender in pale-green glass.

Dark-red dianthus spraying out of a basket.

Six single dark-red roses each set in a glass bowl for centre of table.

Dark-red carnations, white lupins and cornflowers in a grey bowl.

Pale-pink poppies, marguerites and cornflowers.

August

Wild grasses, ox-eyed daisies and cornflowers arranged in a big basket. Water containers, jam jars and a baking tin.

Two cottage bouquets for guest rooms. Sweet williams, marigolds, snapdragons, asters and phlox.

A bowl of roses with clematis twined over wire.

Six brilliant zinnias in a white pottery jug.

Red dahlias in a dark-green jar, arranged so that some of the heads were sprayed out over jar edge.

White and yellow gladioli in an off-white jar.

September

A purple bowl of asters and virginia creeper.

White dahlias with Michaelmas daisies, phlox and Japanese anemones against a white wall, the taller flowers spraying from the centre of dahlias.

Big mauve balls of echinops arranged with ling.

A yellow jug of wheat ears and poppies.

Large dahlias' heads in a floating bowl.

October

Big white chrysanthemums arranged with big sweeping spikes of dark-mauve Michaelmas daisies.
Bramble leaves and trails of bright leaves on wire over bowl of bright berries.
Red and white begonias in a pewter jug.
Yellow bracken, with toadstools in a low bowl.
Short heads of asters and late roses in a ring.

November

Rust-red single chrysanthemums like gigantic daisies. Most effective in bowl of Indian silver.
White chrysanthemums with red berries.
A small table bowl of green glass, with four tea roses and some late violas.

December

A ring of ivy leaves and Christmas roses, holly berries set in a ring with candles for the Christmas table.
Pale-pink curly chrysanthemums in mauve jug with honesty.
Christmas roses in a floating bowl.

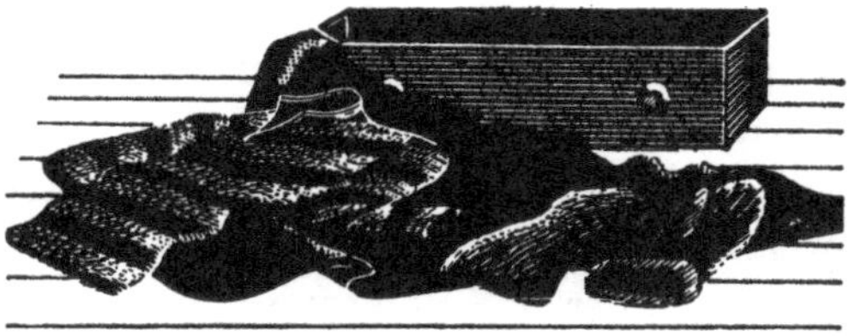

CASTING CLOUTS

'THAT's where the moths collide,' says Mrs Cartwright darkly of the boxroom in the attic, and one has an appalling picture of a sort of Battle of Britain going on up there in the quiet sunny places under the roof. Usually when winter is over, and this more often than not coincides with spring cleaning and the tidying of drawers, I like to put all the thicker garments away, the paper over them sprinkled with D.D.T. powder, everything laid correctly and neat ready for winter again ; coats hung in cellophane bags, rugger shorts and stockings and striped jerseys clean and mended ; mufflers and gloves neatly folded and paired. How pleasant this promises to be, but how much less orderly it is when it actually happens, because no two people in a family ever cast clouts at the same time. Some people never have any to cast, being able to exist in nylon bra and pants throughout the coldest winter. But how much slimmer and younger most people look in the spring. And how agreeable to find, in the trunk where you are putting the fur gloves and scarves and thick pullovers, a length of flowered shantung that you bought at a summer sale last year. Then it seemed a mad extravagance. Now it is seen to have been the most prudent and far-seeing action, and means you can have a new frock for practically nothing—on this year's accounts.

COLLECTING SLUGS

'THE great enemy of the annual is the slug,' as somebody once wisely wrote. I do not know anything more exasperating than to come upon a healthy group of annuals, tender and just slug-high, and find them chewed into green lace. Apart from staying up all night and patrolling the garden, it is difficult to see what can be done at this time of the year except protect the plants as well as you can by ringing them with the various forms of metaldehyde. This, I am thankful to say, is irresistible to slugs. They will travel from afar to taste it, like a dipsomaniac hurrying towards a bottle of whisky. They know it is death to them, but they must have it.

I have been on slug-catching expeditions at night, when my torch plays on the flower beds, and I have the feeling that I am a giantess looking down on a Lilliputian world where innumerable activities are going on that are too small for me to see. If you are lucky on these night jaunts, you catch a slug actually at it, and you imagine the scene as it would be recorded by slow motion camera. The awful mouth of the slug or garden sea-cow, opening on your infant clarkias and godetias. No, it is not to be borne.

I greatly prefer putting little heaps of meta round my best clumps, or, as one garden book suggested, placing them under half-orange skins, held off the ground by a pebble to protect the lethal substance from rain. As you lie in bed you can imagine your enemy advancing on these golden pleasure-domes, and sleep, if you are of vindictive nature, all the better for it.

CHICKEN SURPRISE

Every now and then you want a special dish, and at this time of the year it is possible sometimes to buy a chicken from a farmer friend, or from a friend who just keeps fowls, for less than half your savings for old age.

You might do this with it.

Cut the chicken up and put the six pieces, two wing, two leg and two breast portions to soak in cold salted water. While this is going on fry a sliced onion a pretty golden brown in olive oil, butter or margarine. Take five or six peeled tomatoes, or tinned tomatoes of a brand you have tested, and make a thick sauce out of these, the onions and a pinch of cayenne. Put the pieces of chicken into this sauce and let it stew for an hour, stirring fairly often. It is nice to thicken the stew with yolk of egg and cream, but if you can't, you can thicken it with flour and what creamy milk you have. Pour the thickening over the chicken and tomato sauce. Stir continuously until the sauce thickens. Do not let it boil at this stage.

Meanwhile cook rice, sufficient for the number of guests you expect, and either leave it plain or fry it lightly in butter. Make a bed of rice on a large hot dish ; on this arrange the chicken as nicely as you can, and pour over it the thick sauce. Garnish the dish with halves of green grapes, uncooked green peas, and, if it is the mushroom season, mushrooms. Sprinkle finely chopped and mixed parsley and chives over all just before the dish goes to table.

VISITING A W. W. JACOBS PORT

We are fortunate in East Anglia because the sea is never very far away. You can smell it on high ground twenty miles inland. Great estuaries bite into the land, so that little towns where fishing and boat-building and sailing are the most important things in life are within walking or short driving distance. This is true of much of England, but many people miss the real savour of these places because they think of sandwiches, deck-chairs and bathing as being the seaside. They are, but as early in the year as May there are other things to explore. One of our favourite family excursions involves a visit to a waterside inn, where you can have tea overlooking a tidal river, and watch the big flat-bottomed ferry taking what seems a surprising number of people to and fro. We leave the little town, and between towering banks of dove-grey mud are propelled slowly across to the pebbled stretch of ' hard ' on the other side of the river. The ferryman usually has something interesting to tell us about the boats we see a little farther up by the shipyard. ' She's off to the Nile next week,' he says, pointing to a trim steam yacht, all gleaming white and gold. ' She's been laying-up here all winter.'

On the other side we cross some salty fields to the next

little town, whose waterfront spreads in a bright line of ochre, russet, yellow and cream above the moss-grown mud-rooted piles. There is a lot to look at here, and we wander along slowly peering through the gates of the shipyard, and into the fish-smelling noisy doors of a fish-canning factory. A little farther on elegant eighteenth-century bow-fronted cottages, from which one feels a Jane Austen heroine might at any moment come out, show rooms which either have been luxuriously transformed by seasonal yacht-owning tenants, or remain, with old maps and rainbow hand-knitted rugs in high-backed chairs, as they must have been for seamen to come home to for over a hundred years. Up a side street an inn sign creaks, and we remember all the tales of smuggling we have heard about this place. The cellars in so many waterside towns are noted for their spaciousness, and just occasionally one can find an old man who can tell you about his grandfather, who used to tell stories of the East Coast marshes which were so fearful that they almost have to be repeated in whispers as he leans towards you on the hull he is painting. W. W. Jacobs's night watchman once said : ' Most relations run away with the idea that a sailorman has been knocking about 'arf the world just to bring them 'ome presents.' Looking into the sitting-rooms of so many of these waterside cottages, always open, except in the worst weather, to let in the salt wind and the glitter of salt water, one feels that these relations have been successful. Here are relics of trips to far-away places : panoramas of the Bay of Naples, the moon and navigation lights made of mother of pearl ; China Dutch windmills which may be salt cellars, flower vases or camouflaged tape measures ; cup and plates printed with ' Oslo ' above a forest of masts and incredibly blue water. Richard and Roddy once bought a ship in a bottle from a sailor, and it is a great treasure. Any man who works with boats tries his hand at a model, and many of them, even in this machine age, are experts. They are always very good about telling children how to achieve this seeming miracle.

Perhaps while we have been exploring the waterfront the tide will have risen, and while we wait to go across the second ferry we read the list of ferry charges on the weather-beaten board.

1 Dog	1d
1 Goat	2d
Doctor calling for ferry at night	2s 6d
1 Bicycle	4d

LONDON SPRING

The rounded buses loom through softest blue,
The pavement smells of dust and of narcissus too,
The awnings stretch like petals in the sun,
And even the oldest taxis glitter as they run.

Over the sooted secret garden walls
As in another Eden cherry-blossom falls,
Lithe under shadowy lilacs steal the cats
And even the oldest ladies tilt their summery hats.

FRANCES CORNFORD

DELIGHT IN DISORDER

A sweet disorder in the dresse
Kindles in cloathes a wantonnesse :
A lawne about the shoulders thrown
Into a fine distraction :
An erring lace, which here and there
Enthralls the crimson stomacher :
A cuffe neglectfull, and thereby
Ribbands to flow confusedly :
A winning wave (deserving note)
In the tempestuous petticote :
A carelesse shooe-string, in whose tye
I see a wilde civility :
Doe more bewitch me, than when art
Is too precise in every part.

ROBERT HERRICK

THE PIN

'Dear me! what signifies a pin!
I'll leave it on the floor;
My pincushion has others in,
Mamma has plenty more:
A miser will I never be,'
Said little heedless Emily.

Next day a party was to ride,
To see an air-balloon!
And all the company beside
Were dress'd and ready soon:
But she, poor girl, she could not stir,
For just a pin to finish her.

'Twas vainly now, with eye and hand,
She did to search begin;
There was not one—not one, the band
Of her pelisse to pin!
She cut her pincushion in two,
But not a pin had slidden through!

At last, as hunting on the floor,
Over a crack she lay,
The carriage rattled to the door,
Then rattled fast away.
Poor Emily! she was not in,
For want of just—a single pin!

JANE and ANN TAYLOR, 1814

June

June. *At the Full of the Moon, this Month and next, gather your Herbs to keep dry for the whole year. Set Rosemary and Gillyflowers, sow Lettice and Radish, three or four days after the Full, and they will not run to Seed. Shear your Sheep, the Moon increasing.*

Take heed of cutting Herbs or Flowers with your Knife, but rather gather them with your fingers. Let honest moderate Labour and Excersise, procure your Sweat. Use thin and light Diet and chaste thoughts tend to help. Lie not unadvisedly on the Ground or over-hastily drink.

Distilling of Roses and making of Syrrups and Conserves are now in prime : use a light and thin Diet for the Stomach is weaker now than in the former Months : clarified Whay boiled with cold herbs very wholesome.

British Merlin, 1677

ENTERTAINING FOREIGN VISITORS

SUBCONSCIOUSLY one gets so used to the feeling that if other people are not English it is a disadvantage they can't help, that it does you all the good in the world to see a certain curious gleam come into the foreign eye of the visitor in your home. This can be interpreted to mean that for the moment you are Exhibit A.

The person who is looking at you has paid good money, often a great deal of it, to come across the world to see the Houses of Parliament, Stratford-on-Avon, and you pouring out tea. *You* are filling up the parts of the itinerary known as ' viewing the natives in their natural background.' When the visitor returns to his London hotel, and, if he is the earnest type of traveller who keeps a diary, he will put you and your drawing-room down in detail so that he can tell others at home how it was at that English tea or luncheon party. Fair enough. You remember writing such descriptions yourself in Switzerland, Germany, India.

Usually, and fortunately, it is only after the visitors have gone that you remember this fact, but it always gives you the same mild surprise. By then you are wishing that you could have provided a few more interesting details for the diary entry, but you console yourself by remembering that tomato sandwiches and coffee-nut cake are not eaten at four-thirty in the afternoon all over the world. Most likely even the cups and plates you used were of considerable interest.

It is not always easy to put people who have perhaps never stayed in an English home before at their ease, but if you are really pleased to have a foreign visitor, and show it, then he is usually very pleased to be there, and shows it too.

A very charming Finnish girl stayed here once, who had just taken her finals in law in Helsinki. Her family had suffered a great deal during the war, and her studies had gone on against a background of difficulties which would have made most girls give up. I think she must certainly have found many English women smug and inexperienced. When I showed her to her room she said, 'Is all this for me?' I suppose the large airy room set aside for one person seemed to her extraordinary. She walked round it and looked at the flowers and smiled at me in a way I found touching. She had a brilliant mind, and was learning English rapidly. She could already speak French and German as well as her own language and Swedish. The Finnish women, she told me, all take it for granted that once their child-bearing period is over they will return to practice the profession or trade they were trained for. How sane that is! Now she is the legal representative for thousands of women employed by a big timber firm.

Usually for people from another country it is best to go straight ahead and have the meals you would prepare for English guests, but in the case of the Hindu barrister who was a strict vegetarian a vegetable curry seemed to be the answer. Five years of solid practice since Charles's return from India has made me an experienced curry maker. Certainly the dish I make now is not the same as the one I called curry before the war. I always used, for instance, to make the cardinal error of not cooking the curry powder enough. This should be added to the frying meat right at the beginning of the process. If you don't do this your curry can have a most crude and disappointing taste. It is a mistake, too, to think that the goodness of the curry depends on its hotness. This degree of hotness varies apparently all over India, and the important thing is that the finished dish should have a subtle flavour. This is achieved in various ways, some of them not easy to achieve here, as we cannot easily buy the correct spices, but one of the most important ways is to add a squeeze of lemon to the curry just before you serve it. Coconut also does a lot for it, if you can grate half a fresh coconut into your curry early on in its cooking well and good. If you can't, then dessicated coconut will do, but do add it early in the cooking. Ground almonds can be used instead of coconut. Onions, cherries, chopped apple, raisins, sultanas, diced carrot, peas, tomatoes, shredded cabbage can all form part of a vegetable curry.

The worst thing about this delectable dish, from the cook's point of view, is that the kitchen is apt to assume a Victorian air with many, many dirty pans waiting to be washed. The best thing from the guest's point of view is that it is so interesting. By the time you have tried and passed round all the little side dishes that go with curry the ice, if any, is well broken. To regard curry as a means of using up odd scraps is a sin. All the ingredients should be as fresh and spicy as possible if you want to please people. Remember the dish of sliced banana, the chutney (two sorts if possible), the fried or crisped potatoes (you don't want many of these as rice is the chief accompaniment—but what you have should be crisp), the poppadums and Bombay duck. These last are now obtainable in England, even outside Soho. Poppadums are very thin spiced wafers which are warmed in the oven and broken over the curry. Bombay duck is dried fish. These extras are not necessary, but nice.

It doesn't seem possible to make real chupatties—the flat dry pancakes which are eaten with curry in India—but you can make a very good substitute yourself. Make a stiff dough out of 4 oz. flour, a tiny piece of lard, and salt. Mix with milk. Roll out and beat, fold, roll and beat again. Cut into pieces and roll to paper thinness. Bake in a hot oven for 3 or 4 minutes. The plainness and dryness of these biscuits or pancakes make a necessary contrast to the richness of the curry, for it is rich if you have started off by frying the meat and vegetables in margarine or butter or salad oil.

After all that it seems necessary to add that the Hindu barrister liked the vegetable curry I made for him, and ate it with a pleasure that I don't think can have been feigned.

He was a determined sightseer, so that entertaining him was almost too easy.

'What famous poet has lived in this town ?' he asked.

This town has not got a past strewn with poets, but we murmured that 'Twinkle Twinkle Little Star' had been written here, and that there was a plaque to commemorate the fact that Jane and Ann Taylor had lived in a house in one of the more picturesque parts of the town.

'I would much like to see it,' he said, so we took him to the tiny ochre-yellow tip-tilted house.

'Another work by these authors I remember,' he said, 'from my early English school books. This is it :

> Thank you, pretty cow, that made
> Pleasant milk to soak my bread.
> Every day and every night
> Warm, and fresh, and sweet and white.'

I remembered, with a feeling that at any moment the situation might get beyond control, that appreciation of cows figured largely in the Hindu religion, but since he had brought the subject up himself I couldn't see that there was any harm in pursuing it a little further.

'Another English book for children has a poem about a cow in it,' I said. 'You'll know it, perhaps. *A Child's Garden of Verses* by Robert Louis Stevenson.'

'Please recite it to me,' he said, as we climbed the hill away from Jane and Ann Taylor's house.

Luckily I could remember it :

> The friendly cow all red and white,
> I love with all my heart :
> She gives me cream with all her might,
> To eat with apple tart.

'That is a very agreeable rhyme,' he said graciously. 'Perhaps some day you will visit India at the time of Holi. Then you will see the horns of the cows painted, and their necks hung with garlands.'

I said how much I would like this, and so indeed I would, though the excessive remoteness of the possibility seems to make it likely that I will have to put up with cows nearer home standing knee-deep in buttercups as a substitute.

I don't think, among the various visitors we have had from India, and these are now quite a number, that there has been one so determined to learn about England as this one. Like most people visiting England for the first time, he knew a great deal in theory, but attached too much importance to some details about which we had ceased to care.

For instance, he astonished me by asking, with an earnestness which made it impossible to be anything but serious in reply : 'Can you tell me, please, Mrs Currey, when the Homberg hat is worn ?'

'Perhaps my husband can tell you better than I can, I suggested, handing the baby to Charles.

When, during our tour of the castle and the other places of interest in the town, he told us that he planned very shortly to visit Stoke Poges and see the churchyard where

Gray's Elegy was written, I told him that I had never been there, he was surprised and shocked.

'It is an omission that must be rectified,' he told me.

As we happened to be passing a picturesque churchyard at the time, crowded with trees and urns and large tombstones, Charles suggested, with regrettable flippancy, that there was really no need to go there.

'Just look at that tomb with the stone urn on the top,' said Charles. 'When you've seen that you've seen Stoke Poges. Really, it is quite unnecessary to go there.'

'I have always planned to visit Stoke Poges,' said our guest, 'though I am grateful for the suggestion you have made.'

'"The lowing herd winds slowly o'er the lea,"' I said. 'That's what you wish to see.'

'Exactly,' he said. 'The spirit of the place I wish to explore for myself.'

It was amazing, I thought afterwards, how the conversation kept returning to cows. Did English poets write about anything else?

Yes, it is worth while and most illuminating to entertain people from other countries, if only to be able to face with calmness the extraordinary questions they ask.

A young West Indian intellectual who came to talk to Charles about writing showed a great interest in the cakes I had made for tea. I was grateful to him because he talked about his wife. It is always rather difficult for a woman who knows her male guests are married, but fears that any inquiries about their women may be regarded as an intrusion into deep privacies or a personal affront. I know this is becoming less and less so, and our Hindu barrister, who regarded himself as extremely advanced in all his views, told me of his wife's interest in modern painting, and of her desire to see the European galleries, but I have met this complete reticence about women, and on the whole I think it best to behave as if Eastern women do not exist until I am told that they do.

However, the young West Indian was very interesting and interested, and shook his head over the inability of the average West Indian girl to cook at all.

'So you made these cakes yourself! ' he said. 'That is most unusual.'

I assured him that in England it certainly was not. That most Englishwomen could cook. They had to.

'Of course, our girls do not have to do this, that is the trouble,' he said.

Then he looked at me with his very handsome brown eyes and said:

'Are you fond of eating, Mrs Currey?'

It is such questions that are hard to answer. If you answer no, it is a lie. On the other hand if you say yes, you must own to something which you regret. However:

'Yes,' I said. 'Very.'

'I am, too,' he said.

So that was all right.

Even Americans, who are so close to us, like to visit our homes, particularly if they happen to be old homes. Ours is, unfortunately, not quite old enough, though they always like Victorian houses, because they remind them of some they have seen in the older American towns. It is amazing how difficult it is to believe in some things until you have had actual experience of them. One knows about this excessive fondness of Americans for old houses, but it needed the sight of a sophisticated and much-travelled woman journalist, standing in the yard of one of the oldest inns in England, to bring it right home to me.

'I'm not going back to London tonight,' she said ; 'I'm staying right here ! '

It seems rather like falling from the sublime to the ridiculous, remembering her rapture, to add here that while it's best to make no concessions to Americans when you are entertaining them because they are used to elaborate food anyway, it is a good idea to have a plain green salad at most meals at which meat, hot or cold, appears.

Mrs Cartwright, while preparing for these visitors with me, has too much courtesy to express any kind of surprise. In theory she believes in travelling. Her attitude, however, to the whole question might be summed up in her blank expression when I told her that an Indian gentleman who had been in the army with Charles was coming to stay.

'Very well, Mum,' she said, and then added, fixing her eyes on the ceiling, 'How is the lady Finn ? '

THE FIRST BATHE

YOU have, with the sternest possible resolution, avoided buying the swim suits the sirens in the shops offered you. You have avoided the Bikini type, and the roses and carnations scattered on white satin. You have remembered all the stern words about mutton dressed up as lamb. You have bought—wincing a little at how much it cost—regrettably prices are higher for mutton than lamb—a navy-blue swim suit, which, so the mirror assures you, tones you down, does not emphasise, in fact does what it can for you.

The next hurdle to be got over is the recurring doubt as to whether you want to bathe at all, even if the sun is brilliant. Reminding yourself of your sea-loving ancestors, you finally get over that.

Then what joy to swing up and down, lapped round by astringent coolness, to look at the sky as you float and realise that if you are lucky there will be more of this during the coming month. And afterwards the delicious langour (paid for tomorrow when you feel a little stiff) that is perfection.

LOOKING YOUR PASSPORT IN THE FACE

EVEN the passport official at the Labour Exchange who laughed when he looked at your passport photograph is not comfort enough. His words, 'Even for a passport photograph this is bad,' though balm, are not balm enough. In your last passport photograph you looked like a marshmallow—the spongy sweet, not the flower. But this new effort, admittedly taken by flashlight and just after 'flu, makes you understand why visas are sometimes held up. If you were responsible for the well-being of your country, you think, would you let this obviously low-type, this hollow-eyed, false and hard-living woman in? Especially when her profession is *romancière? Certainement, non.*

And the unkindest cut of all comes when your young son looks at it, and says, 'I don't think it's so bad.'

STRAWBERRY SHORTCAKE

THIS is wonderful eaten outside by a flowery garden border, or in a punt, or in a cool flower-decorated room—or by the kitchen table if the worst comes to the worst.

Ingredients

½ lb. Flour	*1 lb. Strawberries*
4½ oz. Margarine	*Cream or (if preferred) 2 oz. butter, 2 oz. icing sugar for butter icing*
1 Yolk of egg	*Chopped nuts (optional)*
Pinch of baking powder	
½ oz. Ground almonds	

Method

Cream butter and sugar, add yolk of egg and mix thoroughly. Add flour, ground almonds and baking powder. Divide into three, and roll into rounds about ¼ inch thick. Prick and bake in a moderate oven until golden brown.

Crush strawberries lightly, add sugar and a little cream. Put a layer of this mixture on the bottom round of shortcake, cover with next round and repeat.

June Recipe

A layer of butter icing, moistened with a few crushed strawberries, makes a good anchorage for the halved strawberries with which the top of the cake must be covered. If you are all out for splendour with this cake you can cover with whipped cream and chopped nuts. Then it *is* a cake.

VISIT TO A NORMAN KEEP

THERE is something particularly fascinating to children about this particular form of historical monument. Being confessed savages they get great pleasure from thinking how much more interesting England was when it was divided into armed camps, and the routine duties for the day included an hour or two of watching for approaching enemies from a good high tower.

Castle Hedingham is our nearest treat of this kind. Whenever I see it I always think of Osbert Lancaster's story, *The Saracen's Head*, which is listed among our favourite historical writings. At the beginning of this incomparable story he writes : ' William de Littlehampton's principal residence was the castle of Courantsdair, a large, prominently situated building completely equipped with drawbridge, moat, bailey, keep, posterns, dungeons and all the usual twelfth-century fittings, and enjoying a magnificent view of the South Downs and English Channel. Though immensely strong, it had already been built over a hundred years, and unfortunately even by twelfth-century standards was considered more than a little uncomfortable. The fire smoked without stopping, the wind whistled through the great wall through a dozen cracks, and none of the window shutters fitted properly, which was all the more noticeable as none of the windows had any glass.'

I don't suppose there are many buildings in England that can compare with this castle keep at Hedingham. From this village of Castle Hedingham, so much the film village that one almost expects a yokel in a smock to come out between the nodding hollyhocks, the great keep rises from its steep flat-topped mound. There are no gateways, barbicans, pantries, brewhouses, granaries round the keep now. These are represented by grass-grown mounds, but the public are allowed to use the great moat for Sunday walks, and it is easy to imagine what a formidable barrier this was. In 1917 the floors of the castle keep were destroyed by fire, but new floors have been added, and now it is possible to climb up through five stories to the leaded roof where fire watching was done every night during the last war. This keep, although so much of the magnificent old furniture was destroyed by the fire, is one of the best I know for giving a clear picture of the life of the keep as it must have been in the twelfth century. From the entrance hall you climb a stair, which was built for step-by-step defence, to the great audience hall ; from there to the gallery floor, which makes a sort of triforium round the audience chambers; from that to the fourth floor, the living and sleeping quarters of the garrison ; and from a door in the north-west turret on that floor you reach the roof.

Children, if taken there, dart in and out of the various alcoves on each floor like rabbits, and want to know what each was used for. Here is the incredibly small room, or rather niche, in which Queen Matilda is said to have died, and there are all the other crude and comfortless niches cut out of the great walls which provided the only kind of privacy there was in those days. A child appreciates the bare architectural statement of a Norman keep far more than the graceful elaborations of later centuries. He likes its defended, savage sturdy air, and you will find wants to know, or is eager to tell you, just what the keep was like when singlestick, boxing, archery and tilting were going on in the tilt yard below.

Among other castles with keeps where it is easy to recapture this delightful boiling-oil atmosphere are Arundel Castle, Sussex ; Allington Castle near Maidstone ; Castle Rising, Norfolk ; Keep Tower of Rochester ; Stokesay Castle, Shropshire ; Aydon Castle, Northumberland ; Little Wenham Hall, Suffolk ; and Caldicott Castle, Monmouthshire.

THE YOUNG VISITERS

NEXT morning while imbibing his morning tea beneath his pink silken quilt Bernard decided he must marry Ethel with no more delay. I love the girl he said to himself and she must be mine but I somehow feel I can not propose in London it would not be seemly in the city of London. We must go for a day in the country and when surrounded by the gay twittering of the birds and the smell of the cows I will lay my suit at her feet and he waved his arm wildy at the gay thought. Then he sprang from bed and gave a rat tat at Ethel's door.

Are you up my dear he called.

Well not quite said Ethel hastilly jumping from her downy nest.

Be quick cried Bernard I have a plan to spend a day near Windsor Castle and we will take our lunch and spend a happy day.

Oh Hurrah shouted Ethel I shall soon be ready as I had my bath last night so wont wash very much now.

No dont said Bernard and added in a rarther fervent tone through the chink of the door you are fresher than the rose my dear no soap could make you fairer.

Then he dashed off very embarresed to dress. Ethel blushed and felt a bit excited as she heard the words and she put on a new white muslin dress in a fit of high spirits. She looked very beautifull with some red roses in her hat and the dainty red ruge in her cheeks looked quite the thing. Bernard heaved a sigh and his eyes flashed as he beheld her and Ethel thorght to herself what a fine type of manhood he reprisented with his nice thin legs in pale broun trousers and well fitting spats and a red rose in his button hole and rarther a sporting cap which gave him a great air with its quaint check and little flaps to pull down if necessarry. Off they started the envy of all the waiters.

They arrived at Windsor very hot from the jorney and Bernard at once hired a boat to row his beloved up the river. Ethel could not row but she much enjoyed seeing the tough sunburnt arms of Bernard tugging at the oars as she lay among the rich cushons of the dainty boat. She had a rarther lazy nature but Bernard did not know of this. However he soon got dog tired and suggested lunch by the mossy bank.

Oh yes said Ethel quickly opening the sparkling champaigne.

Dont spill any cried Bernard as he carved some chicken.

They eat and drank deeply of the charming viands ending up with merangs and choclates.

Let us now bask under the spreading trees said Bernard in a passiunate tone.

DAISY ASHFORD
(Age 9)

ON A PERFUMED LADY

You say y'are sweet ; how sho'd we know
Whether you be sweet or no ?
From powders and perfumes keep free ;
Then we shall smell how sweet you be.

ROBERT HERRICK

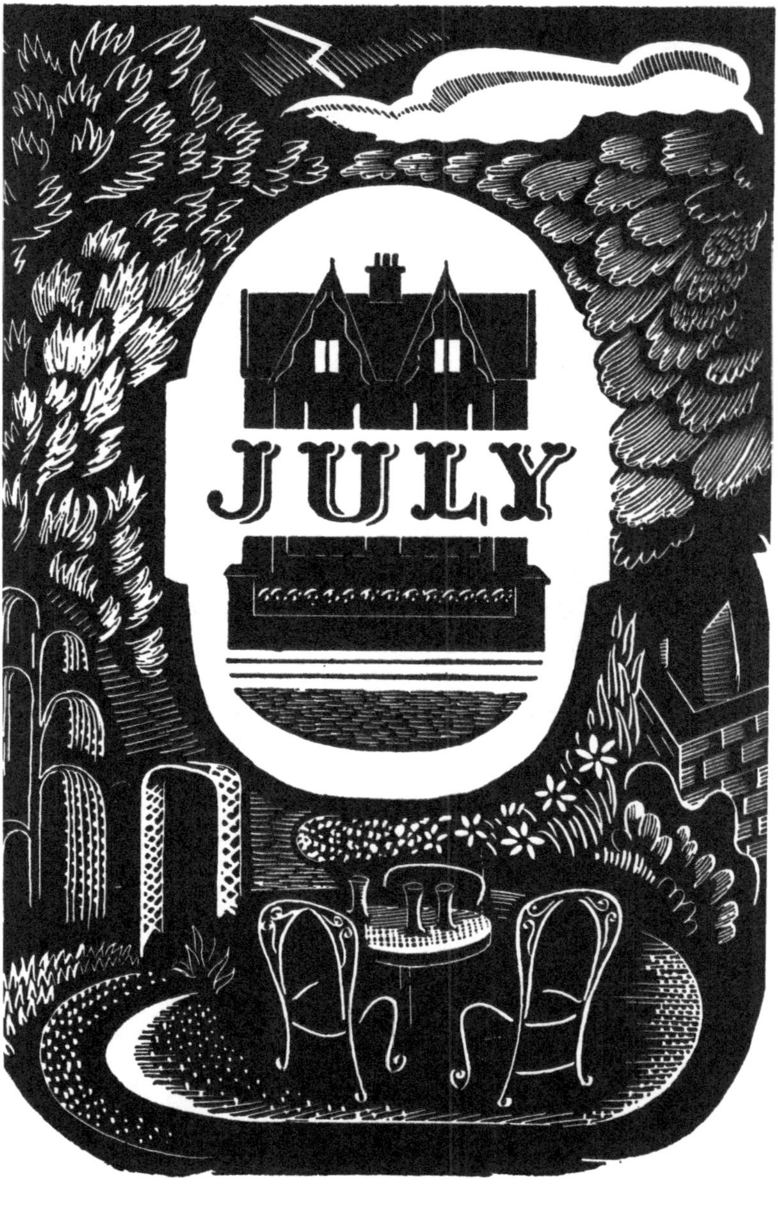
JULY

July. *Get Rue, Wormwood, and Gall, to strew on your Floors to destroy Fleas. At the Full Moon gather Flowers and Seeds, dry your Flowers rather in the shade than in the Sun, which too much exhaleth their vertue ; but to avoid corruption let the Sun heat a little visit them. Beware of violent heat ; and sudden cold, which are the great distempers of this Month and produce a pestilential Diseases : forbear superfluous drinking but eat heartily ; use cold Herbs and Meats ; abstain from Physick. Now the Rivers are more wholesome than the Baths. In time of Pestilence keep your Chamber window shut till the Sun have force of shining. Perfume your Chamber every morning with Tar upon a chafing-dish of coals: use* Carduus Benedictus *boiled, and drank fasting.*

***British Merlin*, 1677**

LIGHTNING INTERVENTION

EVEN if you are not superstitious you sometimes can see very clearly how superstitions come to be accepted. I had never taken the acknowledged partnership of the devil with lightning very seriously until one July afternoon. Then I could understand why Mrs Cartwright prefers to kneel on the floor with her elbows on the ground, her fingers stopping her ears and her eyes closed, hoping by this means to avoid seeing or hearing something she won't like.

It didn't seem a particularly severe storm, although the rain lashed down and the light had some of the yellow gloom of a foggy November morning about it. But suddenly while we were all sitting round and drinking tea a very strange thing happened. There was a flash and a loud clear ominous sound which we variously described as a gigantic whip being cracked, or somebody striking with a stick on a hollow metal pole. None of us was conscious of hearing the usual rumble of thunder.

We all stared at each other, teacups and sandwiches lifted, and then most of us were at the front door looking out to see what had happened, and if what had happened had any connection with us.

And the air was sharply and horribly full of the smell of sulphur and burning.

'You can almost see his black cloak whisking round the corner,' said Charles, adding casually, 'I'll go up and look at the top floor.'

By the time he came back we had established contact with our neighbours, and they indeed could show traces of the Devil's visit.

The whole of the drawing-room, upholstered in pale beige, was palled in black velvety soot.

Now there can be few things more desperately discouraging than to have to set to work to spring clean your drawing-room after tea on a wet Sunday evening in July, and that was only the beginning of our joint troubles.

Naturally the telephones were out of order, but that was quickly rectified. The big chimney stack which served our two houses had evidently been struck, and next day an expert made the hazardous journey up to the dizzy height which the Victorians called a roof, and made an inspection of the stack.

' Can't understand why you haven't all been killed before this,' said the expert cheerfully as he accepted a cup of tea which one felt was the least one could do for somebody who had returned without being killed from that awful climb. ' The stack must have been cracked for years. Amazing somebody sleeping up at the top there hasn't been crowned by a chimney pot before this.'

We thought of all the guests who had slept in such awful danger, and felt we almost ought to send them post-cards of apology for letting them run such risks.

' A stack like that wants keeping an eye on,' said the expert.

Tipping our heads back until they almost met our shoulder blades we agreed that it did.

' But how ? ' I asked.

' A helicopter would be the thing,' said Roddy. ' Then you could hover, and lean out over the edge and keep an eye on it.'

' Nice lot of birds you've got up there,' said the expert. ' They won't like what's coming to them ! '

' What is coming to them ? ' I asked in trepidation, feeling that what was coming to the birds was almost certainly coming to us too.

'They'll have to leave those service flats up there,' he said. 'Whole stack 'ull have to come down.'

'Oh no!' I said.

'Oh yes, madam,' he said. 'There's no two ways about it!'

'But what does that mean?' I asked, thinking of the complicated programme which lay ahead during the next few weeks.

'It means you must get any chimneys you use swept,' he said ruthlessly.

'But they've only just been swept!' I said. 'In late April when the spring cleaning was done. And we've had no fires since.'

'All the same you'd better get them done,' he said ominously, 'to save yourself.'

Thinking of the awful cleansing process that was still going on next door I hastily agreed that I would get the sweep at once.

'What about going away?' I asked. 'We're going down to Somerset in a fortnight.'

'No need to worry about that,' he said. 'It's a long job this. It'll go on for weeks. Might as well get your holiday in before you clear up.'

'Clear up what?' I asked.

'Oh, you never know when you start with stacks,' he said. 'And after all you've got out of it well so far.'

This seemed a good opportunity, I thought, to try out the electric sweep without being disloyal to the good friend who had swept our chimneys for years. He was never able to come at a moment's notice—his favours had to be booked ahead. The electric sweep on the other hand arrived in a matter of hours in an excessively white van. He was a very elegant young man, in a white overall, who seemed to regard chimney sweeping as a sort of job he was doing on the side while he was thinking of something else. He clamped a hood over the fireplace, connected up a sort of sanitary bin arrangement with a power plug, and switched on.

'I'll not be on this job much longer,' he said. 'I'm going back into the R.A.F. ; that is more my line.'

Next day the workmen arrived and stuffed up all the chimneys, seven of them, with old sacks. Meanwhile Mrs Cartwright had given the sitting-room a more than usually thorough clean. The electric sweep, although clean, was not super-human.

'You want to keep your eyes open, Mum,' she said, 'when they take those sacks down. Some of those chimneys ain't been disturbed for years. Might be something in those.'

'Feathers and birds' nests and things ?' I said.

'Those are jacks up there,' said Mrs Cartwright, 'they might have dropped *anything* down.'

Visions of a workman holding out a valuable diamond brooch, or a small tiara, floated before my eyes.

'You want to be about,' she said, 'in case an old sock or a bag comes to light.'

'Well, you must be about for me,' I said.

'I'll see you get your rights,' promised Mrs Cartwright, who cherishes a belief that I am frequently being 'done'.

After that, cheerful workmen perched above our heads for weeks, scaffolding was erected, correspondence with insurance companies took place, a fine dust of concrete and small pebbles cascaded through any window that was open. It was hot weather, so they *were* open. Singing went on up there on the hot roof, and a sort of Sicilian atmosphere of enjoying life to the full seemed to reign around us. Except for the fact that no bottles of Chianti swung from the scaffolding we might have been in Italy. The workmen were sunburnt, and so were the children, who thoroughly enjoyed working the pulley for pulling buckets up and down. Tea flowed around, and there really seemed no reason why we should be anything but glad that the stack had been struck.

Then we went away for a fortnight. When we returned everything seemed to be exactly as it had been except that now the tall chimney pots had been replaced by small fat ones. The workmen were still singing, and the pulley in the garden next door was still being worked ; the only difference was that the fine rain of pebbles and dust had ceased to fall.

And then, quite without warning, on the very morning I was getting ready for an influx of visitors who were arriving on a late evening train from the North, one of the Sicilians came into the kitchen and said :

'Would it be convenient if I took the sacks out of the chimneys today ?'

'Oh yes,' I said, being a little dumb as I had been all through this chimney business. 'I would like to have them out of the way before my visitors arrive tonight.'

'O.K.,' he said smartly. 'I start at the top and work me way down.'

'And no mess, mind,' said Mrs Cartwright, rather sharply I thought. 'That top room's just been done. I'd better go up and put dust sheets over all the beds.'

After a bit, whistling as he came, the Sicilian came downstairs with a large bucket of bits of broken concrete, birds' feathers, an old nest and a dirty sack.

'Not much up there,' he said cheerfully. 'This is the lot from the top room. Of course most of it has fallen lower.'

I was appalled.

As the morning went on I grew more and more so. From behind the sack in the sitting-room about eight large buckets of debris were removed, and from the dining-room the same amount. Each of the bedrooms yielded about four each. The basement was naturally the worst, and from this the Sicilian removed what seemed like a small cartload of rubbish.

I knew why Mrs Cartwright had spoken sharply now. It was only too devastatingly clear. It was too late to send a wire to ask my visitors not to come. They would already have started. The only thing to do was to start a complete cleaning of the house from top to bottom, and trust we would finish it before the train from York came in at 9.30. To this end Mrs Cartwright offered to mobilise her daughter, and with three of us at it there was a possibility that it might be done. If you say was it necessary to clean the house, I can only assure you that it was. True, there was no soot, but every room, and everything in it was covered with gritty dust. You might, if you were short-sighted, and just glanced into the room, have thought there was nothing wrong with it. But along every picture rail, on the top of every book, along every ledge and chair top was a faint gritty overlay.

And the Sicilian had been careful. He was a very nice man, and had, he said, a house-proud wife. He knew what these things meant.

While I was looking out a large enveloping overall I heard Mrs Cartwright say sharply, 'Hi, you just wait with that! Don't you do nothing with that till Mrs Currey comes!'

I went down to the kitchen and found the Sicilian standing with a large grin on his face and a small bag in his hand.

'Look what I've got!' he said.

'Finders ain't keepers,' said Mrs Cartwright.

'You open it, please,' I said.

'Never know what you're going to find in a chimney,' said the Sicilian, fumbling with large fingers at the grimy tape.

'Good as a football, this is,' said Mrs Cartwright, referring to her recurrent dream of some day winning a football pool.

'It's good and heavy,' said the Sicilian.

'Man came round asking if I'd got any gold pieces left the other day,' said Mrs Cartwright. 'If I had, I said, I'd not give them to you.'

Well, of course ours has been, ever since the Romans used it as a sort of retired colony for their officers, a military area. We might have known that whatever was inside the bag would have military significance. The top bag had another bag inside it, and inside that, wrapped in blue paper, were a number of well-preserved ·303 cartridge blanks.

PREPARING THE OUT-OF-DOORS SUPPER

Never say this can't be done if you have a garden with any privacy at all. At the end of a long day it is charming to see a pretty table under the trees, and the space overhead makes for coolness. In hot weather the great thing is to be diverted from remembering that you are hot, and so if you have been able to make one or two unusual long cold drinks during the day the success of your party may, practically, be taken for granted. The only thing that can really spoil it is for you to look hot and worried yourself, so get ready well before, and read a good book on a good bed for an hour before—if you can.

These are the drinks which are practically certain of success. Of course there are hundreds of variations on these, but these four are very good, three inexpensive, one, mint julep, for special occasions.

Iced Coffee. A pint of strong coffee. Chill, if possible, and add creamy milk. Add sugar if you want it. Do *not* put ice in the coffee, but keep in the refrigerator till just before you want it. Some people like soda water added. I like it better topped with thin whisked cream.

Raspberry Cup. Put a pint of raspberries into a saucepan

with two pints of cold water, juice of two lemons, and a teacupful of sugar. Heat till sugar is dissolved, cool, strain, put on ice and serve with whole raspberries and a sprig of verbena on the top.

Mint Julep. Put into a tumbler about a dozen tender shoots of mint, put on these a spoonful of sugar, and then fill it to one-third with equal proportions of brandy and peach brandy. Then take shaved ice and fill the tumbler up.

Cherry Lemonade. To make one quart of lemonade take three lemons, and squeeze them. Put juice into a jug with the sugar. Pour on to this one quart of boiling water and stir. Put into the serving jug with a sprig of mint, ice, a slice or two of fresh lemon and about a dozen halved and stoned cherries.

Having settled your drinks the next thing is to have cool pretty food. What about iced soup to begin with ?

Green Pea Soup. Simmer in a quart of pea or chicken stock one pint of shelled peas and a few pea pods with a little parsley and mint. When tender rub through a sieve. Melt butter in a pan and mix in flour till smooth ; add puree and a little chopped parsley. Chill.

I think as it is likely to be a hostess-cum-cook meal that it is a good idea to have a salad next. You can serve tiny new hot potatoes and chopped mint with this, or a bowl of boiled rice garnished with chopped hard-boiled eggs and chives.

The salad I suggest is a cold broad bean salad, but if you like the idea of this do not use anything but young broad beans. If these are unobtainable very young French or runner beans thinly sliced are good. Mix these with cubes of chopped ham. It is pleasant to decorate this dish with a ring of nasturtium flowers, or, if you must have pink to match the ham, pink cornflowers.

In another dish I suggest you have a plain green salad of lettuce and tomato. Sprinkle with chopped parsley, chervil and tarragon.

The dressing to have with this salad depends really on whether you prefer a plain French dressing of oil and vinegar or a mayonnaise sauce. You can, of course, use a ready-made one, but why not make a good mayonnaise yourself? This way.

Put a yolk of egg into a bowl and beat it for a few seconds, and then add a few drops of salad oil, and beat into the egg. Repeat this addition of oil once or twice, and go on beating and adding oil till the sauce is quite stiff. Add pepper and salt, and a little vinegar until you think the taste is correct.

Mix the beans and diced ham with this just before serving.

July is a good time to have a plain sweet of sugar and fruit, that is, any soft fruits—strawberries, raspberries, currants—put into a serving bowl in layers with castor sugar, and chilled.

Or you might make something a little more ambitious—a fruit mould out of 1 lb. of red currants and ½ lb. of raspberries. To make this you squeeze the juice from the fruit through muslin, bring it to the boil, with ¼ lb. of castor sugar.

Make a thin paste of 1 tablespoonful of cornflour and a little water, and add it to the fruit juice. Bring it to the boil and stir gently till it begins to thicken. Pour into mould and leave to set—about an hour. Turn out and chill, and pour round it whipped cream, or ice cream with nuts in it. A very sightly dish this.

End with cheese and cheese straws made with a good amount of cayenne. This is my favourite recipe for cheese straws:

2 oz. Butter, 2 oz. flour, 3 oz. grated cheese, salt and cayenne. Rub the butter into the flour, add the cheese and roll out. Cut into tiny strips.

If you are worried about your best china and glass being broken just don't use it. A gay checked cloth and earthenware are completely suitable. As long as everything is sparkling and clean and the table and chairs are firm nothing else matters.

KILLING MOTHS

ALTHOUGH told from my earliest years that the best sleep is the earliest sleep, that to read with the book propped crookedly is asking for eye trouble of the worst kind, I hug this bad habit. I find it difficult to understand why those who warn you against this end to the day do not add, 'Moths will tickle your neck with soft little fingers.' I've never read a description of a woman reading in bed in the tropics, perhaps because there they have arranged for all bad habits to be as comfortable as possible, and mosquito nets are provided. In England such amenities are unknown, and in summer reading in bed can be, and often is, utterly spoiled by invading creatures. You can't have the windows closed, at least you feel you can't ; you can't nail down the ninon or net curtains all round because that would stop you closing the window or opening it more. You can't stop reading because you must read; a bad habit is after all a habit, and not easily broken. For the first few minutes you read quickly, feeling it would be good to get in as much as possible before the distractions arrive. The worst are the heavy bombers who zoom in and blunder about, knocking into things, and apparently falling to death, only to rise with an awful whirr if you attempt to touch them. The moths which come and sit on the edge of your pillow, and then with what seems a desperate suicidal flight rise to the light as you pounce, are nearly as bad. And what horror there is in the lace-like fragile things which do a little *pas-de-seul* all down your bare arm. It is not to be borne.

SEA PIE

THIS is a useful item to add to the seaside picnic. You can take it in the tin in which it was baked and cut it up at the meal. It has a thousand and one variations, and is really a savoury custard tart.

Ingredients

Short Crust

½ *lb. Self-raising flour*
4 *oz. Lard*
Salt

Filling

2 *eggs*
Milk

Little chopped onion or chives, sliced and peeled tomatoes, chopped bacon or cooked ham, or slices of sausages or grated cheese

Method

Line a sandwich tin with a short crust pastry and prick the bottom. Make the egg custard, and add some milk to this. You need to be fairly generous with the milk, as the custard should be not too 'eggy,' but don't overdo it. Before you put the custard into the pastry-lined tin you can arrange the filling, an overlapping ring of tomato slices, green peas mixed with meat and onion in the centre. On the other hand you need not arrange the filling, but just mix it. That is a matter of taste. Season well. A few herbs, or celery salt if the filling is cheese, are an improvement. Pour the custard over the filling, allowing about ¼ inch at the top. Bake for half an hour in a moderate oven.

FISHING WITH CHILDREN

THE mesmeric quality of fishing is evident to all who have ever passed along a river bank, and this mesmerism is an agreeable thing if set working on a party of children for whom you are responsible on a hot summer afternoon. Even the most restless child will remain quiet and interested for long periods if it has a fishing rod. And please do not think I am suggesting that you should at once expend a large sum of money on rods, fishing baskets, reels and waders. My suggestion is either that you should expend five shillings on the cheapest possible rod, or, if you would prefer to spend less than this, that you should buy a bamboo rod and a line from an ironmonger for tenpence ; a float, a weight, a hook and a piece of gut from Woolworth's for roughly one shilling the lot ; and assemble the rod yourself. A reel is not essential for children. It can indeed be a positive nuisance.

Children under ten are allowed to fish free in most English rivers, and that is for coarse fish, not for trout, naturally. But if it is necessary to get a licence the cost is negligible. For adults, fishing in the Ouse at Bedford costs two shillings a year, for instance, so for children it will either be free or a matter of pence. Prices in other English rivers are likely to be comparable. If you want to fish on a stretch of river about which you are doubtful, look out for the keeper and ask him, and if he says the children can't fish there ask him where they can. He will nearly always tell you.

AFTER THE EXAMINATION

When someone's happy in a house there shows
A chink of honey-coloured light beneath the bedroom door,
Where once a thunder-purple gloom oozed out across the floor,
And even the stairs smell like an early rose.

FRANCES CORNFORD

WORRY ABOUT MONEY

Wearing worry about money like a hair shirt
I lie down in my bed and wrestle with my angel.

My bank manager could not sanction my continuance for another day,
But life itself wakes me each morning, and love

Urges me to give although I have no money
In the bank at this moment, and ought properly

To cease to exist in a world where poverty
Is a shameful and ridiculous offence.

Having no-one to advise me, I open the Bible
And shut my eyes and put my finger on a text

And read that the widow with the young son
Must give first to the prophetic genius
From the little there is in the bin of flour and the cruse of oil.

KATHLEEN RAINE

MYSTERIOUS KOR

At once she knew that something was happening—outdoors, in the street, the whole of London, the world. An advance, an extraordinary movement was silently taking place; blue-white beams overflowed from it, silting, dropping round the edges of the muffling black-out curtains. When, starting up, she knocked a fold of the curtain, a beam like a mouse ran across her bed. A searchlight, the most powerful of all time, might have been turned full and steady upon her defended window; finding flaws in the black-out stuff, it made veins and stars. Once gained by this idea of pressure she could not lie down again; she sat tautly, drawn-up knees touching her breasts, and asked herself if there was anything she should do. She parted the curtains, opened them slowly wider, looked out—and was face to face with the moon.

Elizabeth Bowen

AUGUST

August. *Now with thankfulness reap your desired Harvest. Sow Winter Herbs in the New of the Moon. Esteem fair weather as precious, and Mispend it not. Gather Garden Seeds near the Full. Use moderate Diet, forbear to sleep presently after Meat. Take heed of sudden cold after heat.*

Beware of Physick and Blood-letting in the Dog Days, if the Air be hot ; otherwise, if occasion require, you may safely make use thereof. Now Moderate Diet is best, beware of Surfiets, Heats, Colds, for Plurisies are ingendred thereby. Use not to sleep much, especially in the afternoon, for that brings opilations, headaches, Agues, and Cathars ; and all noxious distempers of the same kind. Red Wine, Claret are excellent Remedies for Children against the Worms. ***British Merlin, 1677***

May 30th. Pierre arrived today. He is small, thin and bright-faced, his eyes dark brown and large. The last fact is not surprising, for this morning he flew from Paris to London airport. Yesterday he flew from Algiers to Paris. His leather satchel has 'Air France' stencilled on it. A terrifying business at eleven to come to England, alone, unable to speak much English, and to settle into a house of strange people. He shook hands gravely with us all. '*Je suis très bien arrivé.*'

Tonight we will make the bed early.

While his bath is running we unpack. He, in theory, helps me, but wanders off to sail boats in the bath with Roddy.

Pierre's mother has written asking me if we will buy him 'a little English flannel and a little English cap.' Viewing his many pairs of beautifully cut shorts, his jackets with their well-defined waists and padded shoulders, I know this purchase will be a good idea. Better for him to be mass-produced in English flannels for his own sake. His dressing-gown is a dark cape with a burnous head-covering, and his tooth paste is made by Mr Gibb-Thirbauld, his soap, cellophane-wrapped, is Rosy. He has brought me a beautiful red Moroccan leather writing case.

He is appreciative of his blue-and-white room, 'ma belle chambre', and we put his stamp collection, his writing case and snapshot albums, his diary between book-ends. After he is ready for bed he appears in the sitting-room, and shakes hands with everybody. '*Bonsoir, Madame ; bonsoir, Monsieur.*'

June 1st. After twenty-four hours with Pierre, I am grateful to Roddy for his complete naturalness. He makes no concessions, but chatters naturally, and Pierre seems to understand him better than any of us. At bedtime Roddy is a little cast-down, for Pierre was this evening introduced to a group of boys at the school boarding house via a table-tennis game. Some of them laughed at Pierre. I explain, or try to, that this is ignorance, and Roddy must remember how funny these boys would look to the boys of Pierre's Lycée. 'One of the jokes was smashing,' says Roddy, 'and of course I couldn't laugh at it.' Roddy is experiencing the first trials of divided loyalties. This incident is treated very firmly indeed by the headmaster, and after this, no doubt, Pierre, who is a friendly boy, will get on very well.

June 2nd. Today Pierre and I go shopping. This child—I wish I could feel that my own children would do the same in a foreign country—asks me the name of every shop we pass—and seems to remember it.

At the Food Office the tempo slows as usual. A girl with blood-red finger nails and many tinkling bangles writes what appears to be a full-length novel about Pierre. After signing his name twice, and attempting the year in English beginning 'one thousand,' and then faltering, he retires to a window seat and watches from a distance, exhausted, as everybody is, sooner or later, by English form-filling. He is joined by a small fat English child, who refuses to be discouraged when Pierre does not reply to any of his comments. This particualr brand of child has the twin disadvantages of being both a baby and local. His mother finally ends the misalliance by shouting from the counter, 'Don't keep on at him, dear. He can't understand a word you say! He doesn't talk English like you do!' One feels like adding that we hope he never will. Everybody welcomes this diversion from Food Office tedium and looks sentimentally at Pierre.

The woman next to me has just arrived from Stellenbosch, of all unlikely places, and is receiving permission on paper to become an English citizen again ; she says to me with a sigh : 'I really don't know why we keep on coming back to England.'

Pierre and I finally emerge, tired but triumphant. Rain is slanting through sunshine on to the irises in the yard of the church with the Saxon arch.

At the coiffeuse, my hairdresser, elegantly blonde, looks with great interest on Pierre, who charms her with his little French bow, and elegant way of shaking hands.

The outfitter says, looking at Pierre's clothes : 'We English cutters are really the most conservative in the world.' I foil his desire to sell us a suit rather too big. Pierre wants to look English, but there is no need for him to look as English as all that.

In another department I explain that we wish Pierre to appear much the same as other boys in the school to which he goes tomorrow. 'Well, he couldn't wish to do anything better,' says the assistant firmly. This remark is, luckily, beyond Pierre's English at the moment.

The equivalent of Pierre's *hôtel de ville*, the town hall, looks attractive today, decorated with geraniums and marguerites, and he is pleased imagining no doubt that it always looks so. We go to lunch at the cafeteria where I often go myself while shopping ; Pierre is delighted with the novelty of the big room, which is genuinely old and a clever adaptation of the kitchen of a Dutch merchant's house—hooks still hang from the ceiling beams for ghostly hams.

Out of the pocket of his mackintosh, as we walk home, Pierre produces two cartons of *confiture—abricot—Air France.*

June 10th. Mrs Cartwright adopts Roddy's technique in

dealing with Pierre. She sweeps him along on an untidy flood of Essex dialect. No quarter given. Out of her rich store of anecdotes she hauls up one of which Pierre reminds her. It concerns her only dealings with the French—or rather one Frenchman—Alphonse, a waiter.

'He worked for five shillings a week and his food, and he was here to learn broken English,' says Mrs Cartwright. 'Every now and again us girls on the kitchen staff used to have a whip round. "Come on, girls, spare a copper for poor Alphonse," I used to say. He was all right was Alphonse, except that he couldn't bear a cat. My gollies, you should have heard the language the night we put the old *chat* in his room. Out of the window goes the *chat*, and down the stairs comes Alphonse after us.'

We are now getting used to the fact that at bedtime, wherever we are, in house or garden, Pierre will wait to shake hands with us before he goes to sleep. If he has missed anybody he is quite likely to rise from his bed to find us. Sewing in the garden on a fine evening I hear, 'Goodnight, Madame,' and there is the small grave figure in immaculate pyjamas standing against a background of wallflowers and pansies. 'I take the warm bath. It is good,' says Pierre. He regards bathing in England less a means of being clean than a sure way of being warm when he goes to bed.

June 21st. Some things are very difficult to explain. 'Sir Delaye' on a letter to his father looks fine, and is the result of hearing the masters at school called 'Sir.' The question of title and every other complication arises. We try to explain the use of Esquire in English. With logical French eyes fixed on you it is not easy. In fact, like so many well-worn customs it sounds fantastic. Pierre is amazed at the slackness of English children. They appear to him not to work at all. At his age he has, at his school here, no homework. In Morocco he does two and a half to three hours a night. 'Sometimes sleep is not easy,' he says. Roddy looks on him as an intellectual giant.

No doubt the reward for this time of what appears to us to be strain comes when the French, though perhaps physically smaller, appear more at home in the world than so many Englishmen—more cognisant with what is happening in spheres outside their own.

'Do we go on picnic today ?'

Our first picnic, on bicycles, to a wood and a tiny church, which is always eagerly visited by the children because one can see there a piece of leathery substance preserved in a glass frame and reputed to be Dane skin, was a great success, and Pierre eagerly asks for more. This request is alternated with, 'May I take photograph ?' Sensing the rather terrifying concentration on a few, very few, matters—the inevitable result of being in a strange land, and at the mercy of other people who are happily at home and on their own stamping ground—we all pose, dog and all, for photographs whenever Pierre asks us to. Now '*Mes sœurs, mes frères, et mon papa et maman*' may see where Pierre is living.

July 1st. Roddy brings out the Red Indian costumes belonging to Richard and himself, and dresses Pierre and himself up. They go off on bikes to the school field. '*Les peaux rouges sur les bicyclettes.*' I greatly enjoy, while Pierre is here, the primness and formality acquired by the slow and liberal translation of some of our casual phrases. Piquancy and logic are added to so much which would be absurd if we had not taken it for granted long ago.

Today Charles broadcasts a short story on the radio, and I give the boys gooseberries to top and tail while we listen.

'It is good. I know he speak, although I do not understand,' says Pierre, and then he adds with a touch of apprehension, 'When does he return from London?' I suppose that disembodied voice gave him a feeling that one of his chief bulwarks against strangeness might forever remain a voice.

Roddy tries him with 'Children's Hour' and 'Wireless comes to Toytown,' but it is far too difficult. The same applies to listening to *Kidnapped* on the radio, though that supplies us with one delicious moment. Charles searches for a phrase to describe 'rough boy'. '*Un garçon brutal*,' says Pierre, and so now '*un garçon brutal*' becomes another family familiar. I manage to solve the problem, temporarily, of Pierre's English reading by placing a whole row of 'Twin Books' in his room. Lucy Fitch Perkins's simple vivid English is just right. Pierre starts with *The French Twins*, and goes on to *The Belgian Twins*, and so on round the world. I only wish I could believe Roddy and Richard would read the French equivalent as quickly and well. I have no illusions on this point, however.

July 12th. Pierre tries very hard to acquire English table manners. He had difficulty at first with a knife, and we are all, in our endeavour to teach him our code, behaving extraordinarily well ourselves. I hope the beautiful courtesy which reigns at our table at present lasts past Pierre's return to Morocco. I am grateful to Pierre for appreciating our simple food so much. 'Our cook,' he says, 'she makes the food good, but *ce n'est pas joli comme ça*,' and he looks with appreciation on a trifle decorated with strawberries and little green sugared leaves. 'French people they do not like English food always,' he says, 'but I think it is good, very good.' This view is no doubt coloured by the fact that he has a tendency to migraine, and rich food does not suit him. It is singularly easy to avoid rich food here, of course, and his inability to eat eggs is a positive advantage. English corn flakes with fruit and cream he loves, and vows that such a dish is unknown at home. We promise him that when we go on a return visit we will take him a large packet.

July 19th. We are going to the swimming pool every day at present, and Pierre, starting as a timid learner, is rapidly becoming carefree and ambitious. 'I make the length,' he says, and soon he does this. Any day now he will be, like Roddy, frogging into the water head first with a soft splash—Roddy's first attempts at diving.

July 21st. On the way to the sea today we see, from the car, a master at the school looking in at an outfitter's window. 'He look, he look, he buy himself a bowler cap!' says Pierre. When we get to the beach Pierre at once asks, 'Can I take ze bath now?' waving at the sea. At the end of the day, looking, for him, sunburnt and rosy, he says, 'I take four baths.' His improvement in swimming is quite spectacular. From 'I make the length' he progresses quickly to 'I make ten.'

August 1st. Pierre brought with him a miniature chess set. On a sunny Sunday afternoon Roddy is diverted from making a caveman's scalping knife to learn chess. Their voices come across the garden. 'Now you want that I eat you?—I eat your horse!' Roddy irately: 'I want to eat something just for once. I'd like to eat the bishop.'

We teach Pierre all the little cherry-stone games in English. 'Tinker, tailor; big house, little house, pigstye, barn; and a family variant: 'Elephant, tiger, lion, fox.' After supper last night Pierre says: 'I am a rich man, and I live in a big house, and keep an elephant. This is a nice life I have.'

August 7th. Tomorrow we travel down to Somerset to stay

in a farmhouse in the Exmoor village near which my father lives. Here Pierre and Richard will meet for the first time, as Richard is going there straight from school. Pierre is workmanlike and sensible in his preparations for the journey, and his camera and knapsack and holdall have a look of neat appropriateness that is in direct opposition to the confusion in other bedrooms in the house.

August 8th. Pierre gives us some minute travel-sickness tablets at intervals on the journey with such an air of happiness at being able to do us a good turn that it is some time before we start saying, 'No, thank you.' When at last we are met at the little West Country station by the taxi man, who knows us all, and drive deep into the hills, his appreciation is immediate and in French. Various members of my family are encountered returning on the road from the post, or from a walk, in the pale-gold light of early evening, and the taxi is stopped twice for Pierre to be introduced. 'Tomorrow,' says Pierre, 'I go to the Grandfather's house—yes?' Richard, who is with one of the parties, gets into the taxi with us and we go on to the farm.

August 12th. Pierre takes photographs of the farm, and of the tractors and animals, and every now and again, from the top of the orchard where I have established a hide-out, I hear voices of one or another of the boys, or of all three, from the farm buildings, or from the steep little fields on the opposite side of the valley where they are helping with the harvest. At the farm the question of eggs arises. It is rather a case of eggs or nothing on so many occasions at a farm that Pierre, after consultation with me, decides to try one or two. He is so much stronger after two and a half months in England that all is well. The triumph over eggs seems complete.

'My fazer say English sweets are the best in the world,'

Pierre tells the village shopkeeper when we are buying our sweet ration, 'but,' he adds with a shrug, and he really does shrug with Gallic expressiveness, 'where are they?' The shopkeeper smiles at him. 'You should have been here when rationing was off,' he says, 'then you might well have asked.' This is, naturally, too much for Pierre's English.

August 15th. Pierre, although he looks so slight and frail, is tough, and has ability to try very hard at anything he undertakes. He walks with us up Dunkery this morning, and back this afternoon all the way. But his outrage when we get back to the farm an hour late for tea and an hour too early for supper, and no food is at once put in front of us, is considerable. 'But this is terrible—terrible,' he says, and sits on the bank opposite the hall door so that he can see the moment the gong is rung. 'Do we eat now?' he says, the moment this occurs.

Watercress grows in the stream below the farm, and Pierre is delighted by this useful provision of nature. '*Ce n'est pas une mauvaise herbe*,' he says with satisfaction, and when he gets back to the farm goes into the kitchen to help the farmer's wife to wash it for tea.

August 18th. He is obviously amazed at some aspects of English sentimentality. On the farm a particular horse which is of great use on the hilly fields, has a mare as companion. Where the horse goes the mare goes too, although she does little; on the other hand the horse does a great deal if the mare is there. Otherwise nothing. The farmer has accepted the compromise, and this evening, seeing the two animals being watered in the yard as we are coming home to supper, we stop and talk to the labourer, and the situation is explained to us. Pierre's eyes flash, and he stamps his sandalled foot.

'I would not have that,' he says, looking at the enormous

mare, who turns to look at him mildly with a spray of silvery drops falling from her lips. 'I would kill her and eat her!'

September 17th. Today we have been for a day in London, myself and four children. We started early because it promised to be difficult to do all we wanted to do. To begin with we took a No. 11 bus from Liverpool Street to Trafalgar Square. There is no better way I know of to introduce children to London than a journey on the top of a No. 11: The Bank of England, Threadneedle Street; the surprising view of St Paul's across the acres of bomb damage; Ludgate Hill; Fleet Street; the Law Courts; Aldwych; the Strand; and finally Trafalgar Square. Pierre is more struck by the traffic than anything else. 'But this is so terrible,' he keeps saying. A man gets on behind us who, of all strange things, pretends to be a monkey. The gibbering sound and his actions are all most realistic, shockingly so. Obviously his idea is to make us laugh and then collect from us. Richard laughs and says to me, 'Pierre will just think he's a typical Englishman.' And actually Pierre's quick glance at the strange creature before he goes back to absorption in the traffic does suggest that he has seen stranger things than this. No doubt his familiarity with street Arabs and their acting makes this nothing new to him. Janet, who is with us today, whispers, 'How do we get past him if he doesn't get off first?' Roddy takes one look at him, and looks quickly away. In a second or two he has another slow look, obviously determined to make sure that what he thought he saw was really there. It is all right. Seeing that we are not providing a good audience the man gets off in Fleet Street.

We do everything. Look in at the National Gallery, walk down Whitehall, get turned out of the entrance to the Foreign Office, look at No. 10, go into the entrance to the House of Commons, visit Westminster, walk along the Embankment to Charing Cross and take a river bus up to the Tower, eating a picnic lunch on the way. After the Tower, St Paul's, yes, right, right to the top just before it closes. Then I count behinds as everybody hangs out as far as he or she can over London.

Everybody is tired after tea in the train, but happily I thought of buying picture papers in the morning which I have reserved till this moment. We have a carriage to ourselves and there is complete silence for half an hour. Then, almost as if a signal has been given, all four children revive completely, and the journey ends in a riot of giggles, jokes, and Roddy doing a devastating imitation of the monkey man on the bus. I'm afraid we are going to see too much of this strange character.

September 15th. Now it is goodbye to Pierre, who flew to Paris today. We say goodbye with regret, as the visit has been a happy one for us all, but he goes back invigorated by our comparatively cool summer ; able to swim and dive well ; complete with 'English flannel' and school cap ; convinced that English children have one long holiday ; and able to speak English so well that for weeks we have not needed to speak particularly slowly for him.

'I hope I can see the edges of England,' says Pierre, as we say goodbye. 'It was foggy when I came, and I would so much like to see the edge. Perhaps I will never see it again.'

'Oh yes, you will !' we tell him, unable to believe, being English, that anybody can ever go away without contemplating a return, if not next year, well, certainly the year after.

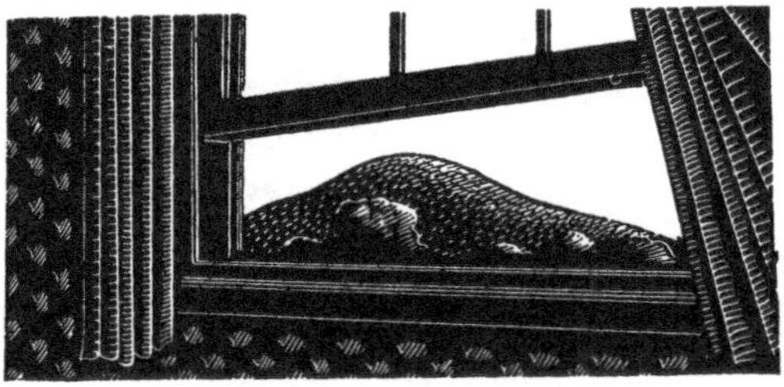

BEING THE LAST DOWN TO BREAKFAST ON HOLIDAY

How charming to be the last, the very last, down to breakfast when you are away on holiday. To lie there hearing everybody else banging on the bathroom door and opening and shutting wardrobes, and to watch the sun growing stronger on the hill beyond the window. To see, after a perfunctory knock, a bright face looking round the door : ' Mummy, you're not still in bed ! You were last yesterday ! You're the most lazy woman on earth ! ' The bathroom may be a little like the beach when the tide has gone out, but it is your undisputed possession. You can wander between it and your room knowing nobody will snatch it from you. You can dress slowly, pause to look out of the window, and brush your hair more thoroughly than you usually have time to do at home. Downstairs they are all pouring their own tea or coffee out and making plans for the day, and you, delightfully, have nothing to do with it. Somebody, when you get down, is sure to say, ' You'll have to hurry ; we want to start in ten minutes,' but you will not have told anybody to hurry at all, and that in itself is a wonderful holiday.

TAKING THE SAND OUT OF SANDWICHES

ONCE, as the elder sister in a family unduly fond of picnics, I vowed I would never cut another sandwich. This vow was taken, if I remember, at the end of a hot summer when we lived by the sea, and everybody had had friends to stay. I expect after this spectacular stand that I forgot all about it. At any rate I must, since my marriage, have cut many thousands more. I suppose I've tried every variant on the sandwich theme, as most women have, the triple, double decker, the roll, the rainbow, the plain, the toasted, the Swedish smörga or open sandwich. They remain to me one of the most satisfactory forms of portable meal, bored though I often am by preparing a large number. The chief thing is to be generous with the filling. For picnics where the sandwiches are the main part of the meal, I find it is better to cut the bread, and butter it at home, and wrap it in a damp napkin, and to take the filling separately. Lettuce in an air-tight container remains crisp, and it is easier to put in thick slices of meat, chicken, hard-boiled eggs or sausage if it is done at the last minute. Slightly untidy sandwiches taste so much better than those which look almost like neat building blocks. Cos lettuce can be used most effectively for a really solid outdoor meal. The long leaves can be filled with slices of meat or cream cheese, and the two placed together in a tin on top of each other, and served round with buttered rolls or plain bread and butter. Little children like very small one-bite sandwiches. They seem to feel that the next time will produce something more exciting than the previous one, and eat more than they usually do. If you have a lot of these left over they make delicious croutons.

But the worst thing, and it is a regular yearly event in August, is to watch somebody drop the largest plate or packet of sandwiches on the beach in soft dry sand. That is why it is such a good idea to divide everything up into small collections, so that one catastrophe does not mean total loss. For it seems quite hopeless to try and get the sand out of sandwiches. You may think you have cut off all the edges, and made a good job of it. You can bet your life that it is only a matter of seconds before some child says, with an air of discovery, ' This one has got sand in it ! '

A SEASIDE CAKE

THERE is nearly always a time in August when you have to prepare a cake specially for children. I give here a recipe for a good butter sponge which may be used in half a dozen different ways. I once used it to make a road-and-car cake for boys. A shallow cake tin provided a good flat surface on which it was easy enough to ice roads and cross-roads, make hedges and signposts of angelica, and fill the roads themselves with the smallest possible models of cars, lorries and vans. A farmyard cake for any small child is always very popular, especially if each child can have an animal for his own afterwards. A round cake can be made into a seaside cake, a yellow beach, blue curling waves, boats on the bay, and perhaps a marzipan lighthouse or pier. A cottage in a flowery garden is more ambitious, but if you bake the cake mixture in two loaf tins, one half the depth of the other, you can shape the roof by cutting off the ends of the smaller one. Then stick the cakes together with jam. You could ice the cottage walls and cover the roof with marzipan and chocolate icing.

Cake Mixture

10 *oz. Flour*	6 *oz. Margarine*
1 *teaspoonful Baking powder*	3 *Eggs*
6 *oz. Sugar*	*Fruit or cherries or nuts*

Method

Cream margarine and sugar, add eggs one by one and beat well. Sieve flour with baking powder, beat and add cherries, add one tablespoonful of warm water, beat again. Cook in a moderate oven.

VISITING CAVES BY WATER

To those who live on the East Coast a cave is almost unknown. Naturally, if you do not early acquire a sophisticated liking for what somebody once called ' much too much sky ' and the changing light on mud flats, you are apt to find the scenery dull. That is why visiting caves by water makes an exquisite excursion. The thing is, if you have anybody in your party who can handle a boat, to take the boat out yourself. If the rocky coast, say of Dorset, Devon, Cornwall, Wales or Yorkshire, is not too dangerous there is usually a fisherman in the nearest harbour who will let you have a boat, or maybe, as we used to do as children, you will have hired an old tub for the period of the holiday. You need to know the local dangers, and the harbourmen will always tell you these in full detail, because if there is anything they hate it is to have to leave their net-mending, or pub-sitting, or herring-eating to come and rescue you if you get into trouble. But what an adventure it is for the younger members of the family if you take your picnic along the rocky coast one calm afternoon, and find a cove or a little stretch of sand which is uninhabited. At low tide there is nearly always such a stretch at the base of cliffs where you can indulge to the full the Englishman's passion for desert islands. The children will put up a flag to say that this piece of England belongs to them. And as long as you leave before the tide comes up it does. As soon as that happens it belongs to the sea. And what is more mysteriously delightful than to search for a cave. Perhaps it is hardly big enough to nose the boat into, but if it is the enchantment is complete. In no other room is there such a silky dancing of light. Here the floor is the sea. Even the children will lie back quietly to watch those pale twists and coils flashing up as from some hidden store of jewels. And here, too, the smell of the sea is strong and intoxicating. Sometimes there are ledges in the walls deep enough to step on to from the boat, and then, of course you must have a torch because in the best caves there may be further tunnels overhead, or right at the back where the light hardly penetrates. Another pleasure, too, is that the rock pools in caves are better than those on the beach because they are less disturbed. Where a pool is in the dark you can shine your torch on to it, and discover a small coloured world of pink shells and waving prune-brown and coral-pink fronds. Sea anenomes and crabs are there, minute and perfect. If it is a large cave you must, of course, go to the end where the water slaps ominously, and is as black as ink, and you feel you are under the world. Somebody once told me that when she was a child she used, with friends, to explore caves in Sark. They used to tie lighted candles to their foreheads and swim into the gloom. Once they found a baby octopus. It is not quite such an all-out adventure that I am suggesting here, but a modification of it.

RECONQUEST

Once a year the East country
Remembers its ancient master :
The fluid corn,
The grey-green swirling oats and luminous barley
Brim up between banked hedges—
The strong tides join and sweep irresistibly over
Houses and telegraph poles
Till only the towered poplars and islanded cathedrals,
Lincoln, Ely,
Look to the Pennines and High Germany.

R. N. CURREY

FORGET-ME-NOT

DURING August I may also notice the corn-flower, and forget-me-not, or marsh mouse-ear, as very observable in our favourite field. The first (*centaurea cyanus*) is exquisitely beautiful. 'Observe the corn-flower,' said the elegant author of *Flora Domestica*, 'what a coronet of sky-blue flowers! every floret a fairy vase, in the depth of which Nature prepares sweet nectar for the butterfly and the bee!' But when these have disappeared, there is beauty also in the winged children, which they have left, rocking each other in its green cradle. In some species, these winged offspring are peculiarly beautiful; they seem like fairies' shuttlecocks, elegantly variegated at the base, and set with delicate feathers of a jet black. And as the corn-flower delights in heat, so the forget-me-not (*myosotis palustris*) fringes a springy bank. Many pleasing associations are connected with this little flower : but the origin of the sentiment, associated with it, is of remote antiquity, and stands briefly thus recorded. Two lovers were loitering on the margin of a lake, during a fine summer's evening, when the damsel espied an attractive cluster of these floral gems growing close to the water, on the bank of an island. She expressed a desire to possess them, and her knight gallantly sprung into the lake, breasted its broad stream, and gathered the wished-for plant ; but alas ! his strength proved unequal, and he could not regain the shore. With one last effort he threw the flowers on the bank, and casting an affectionate look to the affrighted maiden, he exclaimed, ' Forget me not ! ' and sunk to rise no more.

Author of the
Select Female Biographer, 1814

TO THE LIGHTHOUSE

' Yes, of course, if it's fine tomorrow,' said Mrs Ramsey. ' But you'll have to be up with the lark,' she added.

To her son these words conveyed an extraordinary joy, as if it were settled the expedition were bound to take place, and the wonder to which he had looked forward, for years and years it seemed, was, after a night's darkness and a day's sail, within touch. Since he belonged, even at the age of six, to that great clan which cannot keep this feeling separate from that, but must let future prospects, with their joys and sorrows, cloud what is actually at hand, since to such people even in earliest childhood any turn in the wheel of sensation has the power to crystallise and transfix the moment upon which its gloom or radiance rests, James Ramsey, sitting on the floor cutting out pictures from the illustrated catalogue of the Army and Navy Stores, endowed the picture of a refrigerator as his mother spoke with heavenly bliss. It was fringed with joy. The wheelbarrow, the lawnmower, the sound of poplar trees, leaves whitening before rain, rooks cawing, brooms knocking, dresses rustling —all these were so coloured and distinguished in his mind that he had already his private code, his secret language, though he appeared the image of stark and uncompromising severity, with his high forehead and his fierce blue eyes, impeccably candid and pure, frowning slightly at the sight of human fraility, so that his mother, watching him guide his scissors neatly round the refrigerator, imagined him all red and ermine on the Bench or directing a stern and momentous enterprise in some crisis of public affairs.

'But,' said his father, stopping in front of the drawing-room window, 'it won't be fine.'

Had there been an axe handy, a poker or any weapon that would have gashed a hole in his father's breast and killed him there and then, James would have seized it.

VIRGINIA WOOLF

SEPTEMBER

September. *The beginning of this Month, and the End of the Former gather Hops, their Complexion being brown, and the weather fair, and no dew on the ground. Kill Bees, make Verjuice, remove and Set all slips of Flowers, between the two Lady Days ; remove Trees from* September *till* February, *especially in the New of the Moon. The weather warm and the Wind South or West, cut Quick-sets, gather ripe Fruit, Sow Wheat, and Rie, Winter Parsnips Carrots ; and set Roses, Strawberries and Barberries.*

Now as the year declines provide your winter garments hang them on loosly, to prevent that you might after repent of : Good for Physick Phlebotomy.

British Merlin, **1677**

THE AWFUL BASKET OF FRUIT

I REMEMBER my sister laughing at me one day in September as she said : 'You've looked like a doomed woman ever since you heard those plums had arrived ! '

Twenty pounds of plums waiting to be preserved in one way or another for the winter—could anything be more final ! There is never a convenient time for fruit bottling, just as there is rarely a convenient time for having a baby or tidying the larder. There are, unless you are the owner of a canning machine, so many exacting processes to be gone through before you can view the deep purple, the white, the tomato-red or the golden fruits, in bright rows on your shelves. There are the bottles to wash and dry, the clips and bands to sort and sterilize, the fruit to be prepared and washed, and after the bottling is complete there is the period of testing, before you can put the bottles into the store cupboard.

We all preserved fruit and vegetables with such energy during the war that a reaction has set in against this summer pursuit. This is a natural one. In the war if we did not bottle fruit we just had none during the winter. Now, with frozen produce available, and frozen foods always at hand for those who can afford them, the need is less urgent.

Even so, I think any woman who has to provide meals for children is sorry if she does not make an effort in the hot days and look that loaded basket in the face. You learn, as your children grow older, to be discriminating, and to bottle only those fruits which are likely to be popular, and thus save you trouble and money. For instance, the pulping of apples is rarely economic. On the other hand, I am always sorry if I do not bottle a good supply of pears in syrup. It is possible to do this so well that they are quite as nice as the tinned variety, but you must of course make a good sugar syrup first. I always do as many of these as I can for use in fruit salads. The same applies to Morrello cherries. Canned and bottled cherries are very expensive to buy, and yet if, again in syrup, you have bottled some yourself at the time when they are cheapest, you can have fruit salad, cherry pie and cherries with roast duck in the winter. If you like the look of the big white cherries so much better you can bottle those, too, but they are more insipid than cooking cherries. Still they look pretty in salads and fruit cups.

Greengages are another good speculation. Most people like these excessively, and they bottle well—again in syrup. Damsons, especially the little velvet-bloom oval ones which seem to become rarer every year, have such a rich and yet subtle flavour, and I always try to preserve these too.

My family like the mixtures of soft fruit it is possible to bottle in July—red- and black-currants, raspberries, loganberries, cherries and perhaps a few gooseberries. This mixture, if it is not cooked too long, makes a particularly good winter fruit tart.

You must not shirk bottling tomatoes. How do you do them ? To begin with I always make soup, as many bottles as I can possibly get. After that quite the best method I've found is to skin the tomatoes by putting them into very hot water, and then pack them into jars, cramming them in tightly with a little sugar and salt between layers until the juice flows over the top. Then sterilize. This way seems to preserve their full flavour far better than allowing them to float in water. They do not look so globular and beautiful, of course, but they taste wonderful.

Tomato ketchup is also a good speculation, and it is

possible to make it with about one hundred per cent more character than the bought varieties. One of the best batches we ever made had as an ingredient a large tin of tomato jam kindly sent to us from South Africa. This we all loathed, but were too near to the war and the awful shortage of sugar to feel we could throw it away. You can have no idea how difficult that tomato jam was to incorporate into the ketchup. It simply would pervade all the flavourings we could pile into it. We doubled and trebled all the cayenne, ginger and chillies, and even then the sweetness, like that of some women, was all-powerful and all-boring. The more we added the more valuable the ketchup became, and the less able we felt to cast it out. After a time it was so hot that it was impossible to taste it without rushing for a drink. Then, despairing, we bottled it.

Never before, or since, has there been such ketchup. As it cooled its flavour improved, and as it kept it improved still more, and those of our friends who had been to the East found it perfect. I liked it without having been there. We could not, of course, give the recipe to anybody, but there are some things too rare to be repeated. I don't want to give the wrong impression here. It really was a success.

This is the recipe I use when I'm not experimenting with presents from Africa :

6 *lb. Ripe tomatoes*
1 *lb Chopped onion*
1 *pint Vinegar*
½ *lb. Sugar*
1 *oz. Salt*
1 *teaspoonful Allspice*
1 *teaspoonful Cloves*
1 *teaspoonful Cinnamon*
1 *teaspoonful Cayenne*

Cut the tomatoes up with onions and place them in the preserving pan with the salt and vinegar, and simmer until they are soft. Strain the mixture through a sieve, and return the purée to the preserving pan and add the sugar. Continue to simmer till the ketchup starts to thicken, and then add the spices a little at a time, stirring till you like the flavour. You may not want the quantity of spices I have listed above, or you may want more. When the ketchup is reasonably thick—remember it will be thicker cold than hot—put it into hot bottles, seal at once, or allow it to cool slightly, and then fill the bottles and sterilise. It is worth taking extra care over sterilising ketchups. The corks or tops *must* be sterilised first.

One cannot go on bottling plums for ever, and there is a strict limit to the amount of jam one can make. But plum chutney is good and very easy to make. It is a good sweet chutney and goes well with curry.

5 *lb. Plums*	1 *oz. Powdered cinnamon*
2 *lb. Sugar*	1 *oz. Allspice*
3 *oz. Salt*	1 *oz. Bruised mustard seed*
1 *oz. Ground ginger*	1 *quart Vinegar*

Stone and quarter the plums. Add the ingredients to the vinegar and bring to the boil. Then simmer the plums till they are tender, and the mixture is fairly thick.

In the seventeenth-century book of simples I have mentioned earlier I read the following delightful paragraph : 'To keep oranges fresh all ye year, go to ship and take such number of oranges as ye intend to keep out of it before they are washed. Strew two inches of wood ashes finely sifted in the bottom of box or barrel, and then laye the oranges in rowes.'

Preserving those oranges was an adventure, an adventure we can't approach now. But there is a feeling of unusual interest about transforming a quart of ordinary white wine into an exotic orange wine.

Put the peel of two large oranges with 1 lb of lump sugar into 1 quart of white wine. Soak for twelve days, stirring every morning. Strain and cork down.

Yes, I know that twelve days is a long time, but on the other hand everybody will like it so much when it is ready to drink.

Another thing I can never resist is Green Gooseberry Jam. It is such a perfect green if made properly, and people exclaim : 'How do you do it ? Mine always goes pink ! ' The secret lies in the amount of time you boil the fruit when the sugar has been added. This must be five minutes, and no more.

1½ *lb. Gooseberries*	2 *lb. Sugar*
¾ *pint Water*	

Top and tail the gooseberries. Put in a saucepan with water, and boil for twenty minutes. Add sugar, stir till melted, and boil fast for *five minutes only*.

Before we leave gooseberries there is muscatel fruit syrup. This is a good thing to use as a basis for fruit cups during the winter. It adds a delicious fragrance to the cup.

1½ *lb. Granulated sugar*	2 *lb. Green gooseberries*
¾ *pint of Water*	8 *to* 10 *Elder-flowers*

Make a syrup of sugar and water, and add the gooseberries. Simmer, and try not to break the fruit. Add elderflowers and continue to simmer for another five minutes. Strain through a piece of muslin. Bottle and sterilise for twenty to thirty minutes. You can use the gooseberries for a fool, perhaps.

If you really enjoy this delicious muscat flavour and have still more gooseberries you don't know what to do with, then gooseberry jelly is worth trying. Add 1 lb. of sugar to 1 pint of strained gooseberry juice. Tie half a dozen heads of elder-flowers in a bag, and put it into the jelly when it is boiling.

Sometimes in attempts to be thrifty one goes too far, as, notably, a friend and myself once did when making strawberry jam. Cutting out the middle man is excellent if one can do it, and living on the edge of a market-garden area it is possible to go and buy fruit straight from the fields. One excursion of this type we made in search of strawberries transformed our cheap strawberry jam into a costly preserve which we hardly dared to eat. To begin with, a mistake was made in the weighing which we didn't discover until we were making the jam. That mistake was bad enough. The second catastrophe occurred when, still happily imagining that we had obtained fruit cheaply, we stopped the car by the roadside to go into a plantation to pick white and red campion. While we were doing that, and enjoying the pleasant afternoon, a purse containing about three pounds was taken from the car seat. Oh yes, we hadn't locked the car, and the road was out of sight while we picked the flowers.

That jam cost about eight shillings a pound.

I suppose every true Englishwoman feels she has let down her race if she does not go out black-berrying at least once every autumn. I personally like blackberries best eaten warm off the bush. To wander along a hedge and just eat the best you can see is a pleasant way to spend an afternoon. And powerful good for you, too, as old country people say. If you don't want to preserve the berries then you should collect at least enough to make a delectable summer pudding. This can be done by lining a basin with sliced bread and pouring into the bowl stewed blackberries, covering the fruit with more sliced bread and leaving the whole to cool with a weighted saucer on top. Also a bowl of sugared fruit for dessert eaten with little fingers of cinnamon toast is delightful—bottled blackberries keep their flavour better than most fruits. There is something piquant about eating blackberry-and-apple tart with cream while a January snowstorm is raging outside your window.

Mulberry jelly is a favourite of ours—made exactly like blackberry jelly. But mulberry-picking defies all description. No other fruit is so messy, so gory. I have often toyed with the idea, after picking a pound or two, of wandering along a main road with my mulberry-stained hands held in front of me and a vacant expression on my face. I wonder just how long it would be before I was conducted kindly but firmly to a police station, and a policeman sent to look for the corpse. I wonder how much one could be fined for such a pastime ? And what would it be called ? ' Disturbing the Peace ? Hindering the Police in the Execution of their Duties ? Or Intent to Deceive ? '

Anyway, what about mushroom ketchup ? Sometimes at the end of this month the hedges are hung with jewelled spider webs, and your feet leave dark marks on dew-grey grass. At such times we should think of ketchup. This is my recipe.

Place dry full-grown mushrooms in a deep earthenware bowl, layering them with salt—about 4 oz. to every 2 lb. of mushrooms.

Leave them in the brine for four days, stirring twice a day, and then place the bowl in the oven and cook gently for about three-quarters of an hour. Strain off the liquor and measure it. To every quart add one teaspoonful of pepper, half a teaspoonful of ginger, half a teaspoonful of mace. A little cinnamon. Simmer in a preserving pan till reduced to about half the original volume, fill into warmed bottles and close at once. You can add a *soupçon* of garlic, if you feel that way.

You see, it is quite impossible to get out of it. You are sure to bottle *something* before the summer is out.

LUNCH ON A TRAY

I ONCE knew a Chinese woman who nostalgically talked about ' the ten best parts ' of meat or of vegetables, and the impossibility of obtaining the equivalents of these dishes in England. You could not have the meat ten best parts here, she complained, because one of the parts of the dish was dried black jellyfish. You could not have the ten-best-parts-of-vegetables because that dish ought to have dumplings.

' Well, at least,' I said, ' you can have dumplings.'

' No,' she said, ' they must be pounded in a mortar for twelve hours.'

However, in spite of this most discouraging beginning, I extracted from her that in the poor sham which served for an English kitchen a ghost of the ten-best-parts-of-vegetables could be conjured up. You could cut up, or assemble together, cauliflower, celery, cabbage heart or a couple of sprouts, a few broad beans, a few spring onions, asparagus, a few green peas and fry these in margarine, stirring all the time. To this you could add a little vegetable or meat extract dissolved in hot water, and fry for another five minutes. Next you could add two tablespoonfuls of stock, and thicken with a little cornflour. This savoury mess could be served with steamed rice. Of course if you could add bamboo shoots this would be getting quite a few steps nearer to the real thing.

This dish, or a further simplification of it, made with different vegetables according to season, is a very good thing for that feminine meal, lunch on a tray. If you are slimming you can boil instead of fry, and you don't have to have the thickening or the rice. If you say that it is just a mess of boiled vegetables then you are right, and with plenty of seasoning it is very good.

SEWING ON NAME TAPES

THERE is something particularly odious about sewing on name tapes. To begin with, it is a staggering thing how, every term, you have so much of this to do. The twelve dozen you ordered at the beginning of your child's boarding-school career soon get reduced to a number of grimy ones which have been lost, and then put into the odd vases and boxes which exist solely as receptacles for things people find on the floor, and don't know what to do with. If there is anything more disheartening than unpicking old name tapes to put on to new garments, it is finding you have no name tapes left and that you have to concoct one of those dreadful tape-and-marking-ink strips which always come out too big. Yes, it is a rotten business altogether. As you stitch you wonder why on earth you are sending your child away to school in order to have those letters beginning every week : 'Nothing much has happened this week. I watched the first XV on Wednesday, and it was a perfectly rotten game.'

Wouldn't it really be better, you think, going through old socks to find a name tape you thought you saw, to have them coming home at four o'clock and saying in answer to your question :

'Did you have a good day ?'

'Pretty foul. We had quite nice stew for lunch, and learnt about the crested grebe in nature, and had smashing history. I had a small cabbage, but not extra small. As a matter of fact you're not allowed an extra small. You can only have a small, and you must eat it.'

BOTTLED TOMATO SOUP

No doubt you have been led by years of reading advertisements to believe you can't make tomato soup as well as the soup canners. You are wrong. This is a wonderful soup. It can be made when tomatoes are cheapest and, if your family is composed of tomato-soup addicts, you can make enough even to satisfy them at very much less than the price of a tin.

Ingredients (these can be doubled or trebled)

5 *lb. Tomatoes*	1 *tablespoonful Sugar*
1 *lb. Onions (or a clove of garlic)*	1 *tablespoonful Salt*
1½ *pints Water*	2 *or* 3 *Chillies*
	1½ *tablespoonful Cornflour*

Method

Cut and boil tomatoes and onions until tender in 1½ pints of water. Rub through sieve, add rest of ingredients, then thicken with cornflour and bottle—following your usual method.

VISITING A CHURCH, WHOSE VILLAGE LEFT IT

WHEN he was eight Richard chose, as his birthday excursion, a visit to a church whose village had left it during the Black Death in 1348. 'I should like to go to the Black Death church,' said Richard. This request is not really as extraordinary as it may seem, for the little grey church standing alone in the middle of a field had been an object of interest to us for a long time when, during the war, we went by train for shopping excursions to Leamington Spa. We had inquired about it, and learnt that this church had, at the time of the plague, been the centre of quite a large village. So many people died there that finally fear drove the rest of the population away from what seemed a doomed spot. They made their homes and founded a new village some miles away. All traces of the houses have gone, of course. During the five hundred years since then, various local families attached themselves for a generation or so to the church. A wall encloses a few ancient graves, and every year a service is held there. But I suppose, sturdy though it is, the little church was never the same after that mass evacuation in the fourteenth century.

We got the key, the biggest I have ever seen, from a cottage across another field. The door creaked with a strange loud creak which reminded me of the moments in films when something strange and terrible is about to be shown to you. The door swings slowly, slowly, and you see. . . .

In this case we saw—greyness. The pews were all of natural English oak which becomes almost silvery grey if left alone, and added to this natural silver was the undisturbed chiffon covering of dust. The ancient trunk for the church deeds at the back of the nave looked as if it was in the process of going back into the earth. The bier, palled with dust, stood by its side. We put the flowers the children had brought on the altar, and we lifted the dusty hanging to look down into the crypt.

Then we went back into the warm autumn sunlight. The warmth enclosed us like a bath as we closed the lamenting door again.

'There's supposed to be a secret passage from here to the inn,' Richard told me. 'That must be a mile. It would be smashing to find it.'

Roddy, who had asked permission to carry the key, which was about half as big as himself, was already refreshing himself with blackberries as we walked back to the cottage. His mouth was purple.

'I wish I could have seen a bat,' he said.

'It is much too lonely, that church,' said Richard. 'Those people should have taken it with them.'

PREFACE TO THE BOOKE OF HUSWIFERIE

Take weapon away, of what force is a man ?
Take huswife from husband, and what is he then ?

As lovers desireth together to dwell,
So husbandrie loveth good huswiferie well.

Though husbandrie seemeth to bring in the gaines,
Yet huswiferie labours seeme equall in paines.

Some respit to husbands the weather may send,
But huswifes affaires have never an end.

THOMAS TUSSER, 1523

CABBAGE HOLIDAY

'The usual parcel from Major Hornblow to the French lady,' and Fifine cursed inwardly when she saw it.

Her first effort at repartee had been followed by the Major with a Lily of the Valley (Return of Happiness), to which she had managed to reply with a Houstania (Content).

Then came a reckless parcel from him containing Lilac (First Emotions of Love), Fleur de Lys (I Burn) and Mezereon (Desire to Please).

Fifine was overcome, and her bedroom was beginning to look like a conservatory. Hesitating between Coronella (Success Crown Your Wishes) and a Convolvulus (Extinguished Hopes), she compromised between the two with a Wild Daisy (I Will Think of It) ; but he hotly returned with a bunch of Diosma (Your Simple Elegance Charms Me), Jasmine (Transport of Joy), and, curiously enough, Stephanotis (Will You Accompany Me to the East ?).

Things were moving too fast. Ordinary conversation could never be so breath-taking, for it was limited firstly by the embarrassing presence of the admirer or admired, and secondly by the lack of eloquence from which many of us suffer, and particularly the Major. She was tempted to send him Fool's Parsley (Silliness), but with the help of the gardener acquired a Diplademia Crassinoda (You Are Too Bold).

There was an awkward silence. At last he broke it, *tout court*, with Monarda Amplexicaulis (Your Whims Are Quite Unbearable). She had to calm him with Eglantine (I Wound to Heal).

It was their first quarrel.

ANTHONY THORNE

OCTOBER
LOT 10
LOT 27

October. *Sow Wheat and Rie, remove Plants and Trees about the New Moon, observing this as a seasonable Secret, that in setting, you carefully place that side to the South and West that were so before you took up the plant: set all kinds of Nuts and Acorns and cut Rose Trees but once in two years, if you intend to have store of Roses.*

The Garments you last Month hung on your backs in jest, now button them close in good earnest, Cloathes you now for prevention for the cold comes insensibly, and fogs oftimes beget a whole Winters cold. Consult with your Tailors as well as Physitians. **British Merlin, 1677**

TAKING THE CHEST UPSTAIRS

PERHAPS you're one of those fortunate women who can go into a furniture saleroom, look round and walk out again, free and untrammelled. I wish I could.

Last time I visited one I bought a carved-oak linen chest of drawers.

When I saw it, lurking between a tomb-like wardrobe and a mahogany tallboy, I knew at once that it was just what Charles and I needed. Smooth-sliding drawers going a long way back. Shallow ones at the top, meant for napkins and mats, and deep ones at the bottom, meant for blankets and sheets. The sort of chest which was made when linen meant six dozen of everything. We merely wanted it for papers, not having, or ever being like to have, that much linen.

Our house is four storeys high, counting the basement, hideous outside, unexpectedly charming inside, and the top floor is reached by the sort of steep stairs Victorian builders fitted in where any sane person would say a rope ladder or nothing. On this top floor is a big many-windowed attic room, remote, almost shout-proof, where we often work. It was for this room that we needed more drawer space for papers. When you have two writers under one roof you are always needing more drawer space. After a bit the papers and the books push you out of the house, but we haven't got to that stage yet.

I was in a hurry, and in any case I was quite sure the bidding would be too high. I asked one of the auctioneer's men to bid up to £20 for me. It didn't seem at all likely that I'd get it for this price, so I went home and forgot all about it.

But next day a gloomy voice told me over the telephone that I hadn't made arrangements to collect oak linen chest, and would I do same at once.

When I saw my bargain again I knew why I had got it. Without the wardrobe and tallboy flanking it it looked as big as a house.

My low spirits were lifted by hearing a man remark, ' Look at that chest ! Lovely thing ! Practically given away. Half the size it would have fetched three times as much.'

Toying with the idea of getting it sawn in half and making some easy money, I went home to tell Charles.

Even when two full-grown men staggered with it into the hall Charles was restrained. One of them remarked, ' Fills the place up nicely ? ' Charles merely agreed that it did.

But when we were left alone with the chest he said :

' It's longer than a piano, and goes farther back.'

' But it's not so high,' I said hastily.

' Now where are you going to put it ? ' he asked.

I told him in the alcove in the study, of course. Surely he knew that. Charles said he had known it till he saw the chest. Then he naturally thought that I must have changed my mind. This chest would not go up one flight of stairs, let alone two.

' But we don't want it anywhere else,' I said.

' One thing is quite certain,' said Charles. ' It cannot go upstairs.'

Finally we took all the drawers out, up-ended it, stopped Roddy and the irrepressible Whack from trying to play houses in it, and after a period of agonising paint-scraping, got it into the dining-room.

' Did you measure the alcove ? ' asked Charles. ' It might go in one of those.'

I had not measured them, and it wouldn't.

We tried it in front of the window.

'It would be all right there,' said Charles, peering at me through the twilight, 'if we had another window.'

We were so exhausted by this time that I suggested we should have a cup of tea. As we sipped I asked Charles if he thought we should make the boys' room on the first floor into a study. I knew Charles had always liked the view from the boys' window.

'All right,' said Charles. 'It looks as if our lives are going to be disorganised by this chest anyway. I don't know whether we can get it past the long mirror. In fact, I'm sure we can't, but if you can manage one end without hurting yourself we'll try. It's not heavy.'

'Only enormous,' said Roddy helpfully.

The tall mirror which takes the height of two floors at the angle of the stairs escaped, but only just.

'Mind the window!' shrieked Roddy.

Concentrating on the mirror we had forgotten the window behind us. Only a last-minute turn by Charles saved what I was by then secretly calling the white elephant from charging through it.

The turn also took the chest onto the first landing.

After sharing a cigarette—we couldn't be bothered to get past the chest to fetch any more—Charles went to look at the boys' room.

'This room is smaller than I thought,' he said. 'I really don't like working in a small room. With the chest in here there wouldn't be room for the big desk and the bookshelves.'

I agreed that there wouldn't be, and looked beyond Charles' shoulder at the attic stairs, thinking how free and happy I had been before I bought the oak chest.

'I do wish that you'd give that idea up,' said Charles, following my eyes.

'I can't,' I said. 'In the study it would be useful, and look charming. Anywhere else it would be a nightmare.'

Charles said I was wasted in civilised life. I ought to be living on the edge of a primeval forest urging some poor idiot to cut a way through it.

For the first five steps of the attic stairs Charles, who was, of course, at the top and most difficult end, kept asking me if I was all right.

'Of course,' I said. 'It's going up like a bird.'

Then it stuck. It even seemed impossible to take it down now. I couldn't see Charles at all. I imagined us feeding him by passing baskets of food up through the front window until workmen came to remove the chest.

'Unless you want me to starve,' said Charles, who seemed to have read my thoughts, 'you'll have to get Richard to saw a way through to me.'

I sat down, the chest looming over me like a close-up view of Snowdon.

At that moment Richard arrived home from school, and Roddy explained, with, I thought, horrible cheerfulness, what had happened.

'And now it's completely stuck,' he said.

'You ought not to have done it this way at all,' Richard told me. 'It's a block-and-tackle job. Heaving the thing up the front of the house would have been far easier. Of course it would have meant taking out the top window.'

I thanked him for the useful hints, and then Charles shouted through the chest :

'I've got an idea ! We'll use the newel post !'

'He sounds as if he's entombed in a mine,' said Richard, looking pleased and interested.

During the next five minutes working blindly like a mole, there were at least two occasions when I wished that Charles would say finally that this was where he gave it all up. But now he was all enthusiasm.

'Ease a little to the left,' said Charles, 'and then, if you can manage it, heave straight. Then when I swivel, you lift and keep close in to the stairs. But don't try it if it's at all difficult.'

I did what I thought he meant.

It was Charles who had the full glory of seeing the chest rise and swivel, and the newel post at the top of the stairs acting as a sort of pivot as it stuck into one of the drawer apertures.

I sat down on the top step, and Charles, panting, leaned over to ask how I felt.

'If,' he said, after being reassured, 'we go to another house at any time, and I am not about when the removers come, tell them how we did it!'

My adventures in salerooms are not often as wholesale as this, because, knowing my weakness, and the positive lust for possession which invades me for short destructive periods, I more often than not keep away from them. What I really like is to go to a sale with somebody who knows the technique of frowning or nodding or lifting the eyebrows, and who will do this for me. Then I am free to observe the behaviour of the crowd, and to speculate on the probable nature of the home which is disintegrating before our eyes.

The people who lived in this house, you think, must have been very fond of pictures and music. You mark down the thin dark little woman on the other side of the auctioneer's table as a probable purchaser for the Iron-frame Upright Pianoforte in Ebonised case by Bechstein. Yes, in her mind she already possesses it, for she has just removed lot 71, four jardinières and two richly decorated two-handled vases from its polished top and put them, none too safely, on top of lot 54, a Shereton-style corner cabinet with cupboard underneath.

Yes, the auctioneer is dealing with the pictures now, and here the jargon is fascinating.

'Large oil painting in gilt frame, copy "Landscape and Figure", and Lot 94, Pair of ditto in ditto "Dogs" and one ditto "Cattle".'

Everybody looks stolid at this, and there are no bids. The ditto in ditto dogs look sadly down at us out of masses of sepia hair.

'Come on, ladies and gentlemen,' says the auctioneer, 'nearly five shillings' worth of firewood at the back!'

Somebody bids 3s. 6d and gets the lot.

The books fetch more, especially the handsome calf-bound volumes. They go, of course, to dealers, who sell them to interior decorators, who are willing to buy any number of old books, regardless of contents. 'They look good, they look old and they give tone,' as one dealer said to me.

'Lot 9, *Dictionary of Universal Biography*, 16 vols., with Rollin's *Ancient History* in red morocco, 8 vols., look nice in a case!' says the auctioneer, and a dealer, yawning a little, buys all that weight of learning for five shillings.

'Lot 110, Fifty volumes of books.'

'Lot 111, Fifty ditto.'

'Lot 112, Large quantity of music.' The feverish little woman gets it for £2, and smiles tremulously, in her mind already torrents of music exquisitely falling.

'Now we'll get on to something more interesting,' says the auctioneer. 'Lot 113, 4 foot Veined walnut bedstead.'

In the background the local second-hand booksellers are already picking up their fifty 'volumes of books.'

The awful indestructibility of possessions is, if you let it, apt to depress you at salerooms, but usually this is countered by one's delight in the humorous behaviour of all those who are the temporary companions of these wise old chests and that 'lacquered pole-screen inlaid mother-o'-pearl and ditto work-table.'

'She'll do those up and sell them to Americans for £50 this summer, you see,' says my neighbour when the pole-screen and ditto work-table are knocked down for £1 10s.

The gambling instinct which is in everybody is satisfied by auction sales. I always remember Richard being madly excited when at the age of eight he bought for the fabulous price of 1s. two pounds of onions (which he disliked) at a garden party auction sale. 'Look what I've *won*, Mummy!' he said.

Won is the operative word. If more than two people are bidding it is enough to drive most usually normal people into a frenzy, and they will gamble away the week's house-keeping money on something they will know as soon as they get outside they really do not want.

One woman I know, who loves salerooms but has little money to spend and a houseful of furniture anyway, spends 5s. a week, or less, never more, at the weekly sale in her town. She prefers this to bridge, and it is amazing what in these odd lots she has picked up. There is an unseen genius presiding over the compilers of auctioneers' catalogues, I am sure, so that you get delicious juxtapositions in odd lots, such as 'sundry spoons, two mounted heads and old tea caddy (broken hinge),' or 'birdseye maple case, box camera, pair of beaded arm wraps,' or 'collection of pressed seaweed, 1 plated swan containing small sundries.'

It is always those small sundries which are irresistible to this 5s. a week gambler. They may be literally anything, she says. Among those odd lots she rates as her most valuable finds a blue Wedgewood jug, three discoloured Georgian silver teaspoons, a seventeenth-century miniature, twelve solid silver buttons, dirty and blackened, and a goblet of pale milky Bristol glass. These precious and beautiful objects have been picked out of masses of rubbish which are ploughed back again into the saleroom.

Years of study of old china, old glass and furniture are needed before you can be a buyer who really knows what is what. But there is no doubt that most women who have natural good taste can quickly learn, and because furniture buying at auction sales is such a gamble, period pieces of elegance, and even considerable value, can be bought at local sales by amateurs in the game. The same applies to second-hand shops. For instance, I recently bought a very nice little pedestal table, about one hundred and fifty years old, I suppose, which I wanted for a bedside table in a guest room. This was only 30s. I am collecting old furniture gradually for this room, and I was very pleased with this little piece which I saw, on a most discouraging day of melting snow and cold damp air, standing among a number of twentieth-century relics of plywood and rexine on the pavement outside a second-hand shop. The shopkeeper said it hadn't been in a sale, but his brother had had it in his front room with a fern on it, and he was buying modern furniture and wanted to get rid of it. I imagine that if it had a fern on it I would want to get rid of it too.

In such ways these treasures arrive. The thing is to know what you want, and have patience. You are often helped to get what you want by such circumstances as a 'flu epidemic, which keeps people away from sales, a local election, a specially cold or wet day—anything. It's a game of chance, and enthralling as all such games are.

TAKING A CHILD TO SEE SHAKESPEARE

WE are very fortunate in our town as we have a good Repertory Company who put on a Shakespeare play fairly regularly, and thus from about the age of nine onwards our children have been able to see productions of Shakespeare which have started them with the idea, which I expect to last them always, that going to see Shakespeare is a major pleasure. Not many people are as lucky as we are in this respect, but even if it takes more effort than I personally have to make, there is nothing more rewarding than making sure your child sees Shakespeare. The complaint that Shakespeare was ruined for people at school by bad teaching is not so often heard now, for the uninspired teacher is helped out by radio, television, the Children's Theatre productions, and the high general level of school productions of Shakespeare. His or her pupils leave school with love of Shakespeare as part of their natural background.

One of the many delightful things about having children is through them to learn so much you have missed. *Julius*

Caesar was one of my gaps, but now that I have been through it, first to tell the story to Roddy before we went, and have taken him to see it, and talked it over afterwards, I begin to see what a gap it was. 'They got the blood made up for them at Boots!' says Roddy after the assassination scene.

Richard writes from school: 'I went on reading Henry V on my own after the lesson, I enjoyed it so much. Could we see it in the holidays at the Old Vic, d'you think?'

And another time:

'We had to pay 2s 6d ourselves if we wanted to see the film of Hamlet, but it was worth it.'

It always is worth it.

CLEANING BRANDY SNAPS OUT OF THE OVEN

I EXPECT many who read this are expert makers of brandy snaps. This paragraph, therefore, is not for you. It is for the woman who might, as I did once on a never-forgotten occasion, make them with self-raising flour. Now the recipe I use for brandy snaps is this :

2 *oz. Butter or margarine*	2 *oz. Sugar*
2 *oz. Treacle*	2 *oz. Flour*

I melt the butter and treacle together over a low light, and add the sugar and flour gradually, and allow the mixture, as I stir it vigorously, to come to the boil. On a greased oven tray I drop teaspoonfuls of the mixture about four inches apart and place the tray in a fast oven for about three minutes. Then I allow the biscuits to cool for about half a minute—no longer or they become quite unbendable—and roll them round a wooden spoon handle. It is no good explaining how to do this. You just have to remember how you like brandy snaps, and try, quickly and lightly—no good brooding—to make them like that.

The above is what I do when I am in my right mind. Observe a woman who is not, and who, full of glad anticipation because, at this chilly time of year, with firelight and twilight mixed for tea, brandy snaps filled with cream will be a treat for everybody, bends to open the oven when the four minutes of cooking are over. If you have never tried to clean stalactites of brandy snaps out of an oven it is one of the experiences of life you can afford to miss. The pale golden sticky substance hangs everywhere, and on the oven sheet is a thin, heaving, unworkable volcanic mass. By the time you have cleaned the oven, cleaned the sink, cleaned the cloth that cleaned the oven, cleaned the trays, burned the toffee-like remains in the boiler, washed your hands, you have decided on scones for tea, and hardly have strength to make those.

PEARS BAKED IN MULBERRY JELLY

This recipe is one which seems to please men a good deal. This is pleasant, as they are so often indifferent to sweets. It is one of those long slow-cooking dishes which should be combined with something else in the oven.

Ingredients

Cooking pears. Either 1 large for everbody, or 2 small, with a few over for seconds

4 oz. Sugar (preferably brown)

Mulberry or blackberry jelly

Cream

Method

Do not peel the pears, but wipe them, cut off stalks and rough places, and generally make them comely. Make a syrup in a saucepan of say two tablespoonfuls of mulberry (we like the slightly exotic flavour of this best), blackberry or blackcurrant jelly, and the sugar. Stir with a wooden spoon until melted. Arrange the pears in a fireproof dish and pour the syrup over them. Cook for four hours at the lowest possible heat, basting the pears every now and again with the syrup. They become delicious with long slow cooking. Add the cream before serving. Can be eaten hot or cold.

A PICNIC WITH THE THRESHERS

OCTOBER may be a little early for this trip, as threshing is done on most farms between October and January, but if you know a farm where the ricks are being threshed and it is within reach by car, or on foot, it makes a wonderful afternoon out for small children. Many is the egg sandwich I have eaten cosily sitting on a pile of straw out of the wind, admiring the bare branches of trees against a cold blue sky, sure in the pleasurable knowledge that for an hour at least the children would be utterly absorbed. Now you know what capacity a child has for staring at one thing for a long time. Here there is plenty to stare at. He can do just that, and be happy, for the noise of a thresher is mesmeric, and there are so many processes going on that he won't want to move far. Perhaps the threshing machine he is watching will let the chaff fall down in and around the machine, and if so there will be a young boy there to keep it from accumulating too thickly. Most of the modern ones have a blower, which sends the chaff fascinatingly up into the sky and away. There is also the business of throwing the sheaves up to the thresher. Usually there are two or three men on this. Most fascinating of all is the elevator which is building the new rick, carrying the wispy golden straw up and dropping it off in a pale cascade. A quiet walk round the unthreshed rick, or the one that is being threshed, will nearly always show, to those who like mice—and this is all small children as far as I know—one or more mouse families on their way out of one home and into another. More likely than not the new home is the rick which the elevator is building a few yards away. Huge mouse families are bred in these straw ricks, and it is interesting to note how the annoyance and perturbation which one would feel oneself at being suddenly turned out of home are clearly visible in the way the mice pause on the edge of the old rick before venturing out, whiskers bristling. One feels almost surprised that they are not carrying a few cooking pots, or a pile of sheets, they look so domesticated and upset.

TAILOR'S PRACTICAL GUIDE

'MR JOHN S— was the son of a clergyman of the established Church of Scotland, who had been in his youth what few people admire in gentlemen of his profession—a dandy. Though he was no longer finical and modish in his own wearing apparel, he might be said almost to have encouraged his sons in their very absurd devotion to show and dress. It was, however, with John, the youngest, that I was chiefly annoyed. It was when light drab greatcoats, with large mother-of-pearl buttons, were the supreme rage of fashion. I had finished such a one to my young gentleman, to be ready for his first season in college. A day or two passed over. Down came my customer with the coat almost entirely unmade. He had, in his own apartments, been trying his hand as an amateur tailor. He had put six plies of strong sail-cloth and packing-paper underneath the breast facings, for he wanted no lapels on his coat. Ply upon ply was superadded over the breast, until the sail-cloth and paper were fully an inch thick. Mr John had stitched the various parts together, as nearly as possible in the manner in which they had been originally made up. He had tried on his greatcoat. As might have been expected it would not button. He was in agony.

'I want,' said he, 'to have my greatcoat to stand out like the jackets of the Yeomanry Cavalry, and the more canvass and paper I put in, the looser becomes the front edge of my coat, and it will not button.'

As well as I could, I explained to him that having forbidden me to put lapels on his coat, it was impossible that it could ever assume the form he desired.

'What is to be done,' said he ; 'can you not put lapels

on it now ? It is only cutting away these button-holes and sewing them on again.'

I was obliged to make new breasts to the greatcoat, with seamed-to lapels. This was done in good time for his departure. Still the garment would not do. It was now too low in the collar. I made a new collar. Again the greatcoat was sent home, but only to come back. This time it was too long in the skirts. This fault was soon remedied. Ten days had only to pass over before Mr John must take his leave. Four of these days elapsed, and with the fifth came the greatcoat and its wearer.

'What is wrong now ?'

'Ha ! this greatcoat of mine is too short in the waist, and the flaps do not come far enough round before and behind.'

This time I asked whether his father had ever seen the garment ! and whether he did not think that it would be as well that his father should know that so much extra expense had been incurred by these various alterations. His answer was 'I was only anxious to show it to him after all the improvements were made on it.'

It was now my time to demur. I told him that by the additional cloth, and the trouble of making various alterations, his greatcoat would now cost nearly as much as two should do.

At this he stared, but instantly added, 'I will pay the extra expense out of my pocket money.'

Forthwith he proffered a sum. What do you think ? Why, exactly five shillings and ninepence !

To conclude this brief sketch of an incident at once typical of the means, the skill and the taste of *THE YOUTH* I have only to add that I had to make a new greatcoat, in accordance with the better opinion of his father, who said,

'Make my son John a greatcoat large enough to outlast his growth for a year, and as much in the fashion as you can ; and if he does not choose to wear that, he may trust alone to his student's gown for keeping out the cold winds of winter.'

ANON., 1850

THE LETTERS OF KATHERINE MANSFIELD

I AM at present being stared at by (1) very old winged beetle, who is evidently looking to see if this is his club or not, and whether there is an octogenarian or two to have a chat with ; (2) three white moths with their little moth's noses pressed as flat as flat can be ; (3) an unknown, with six legs and the appearance of a diminutive lobster ; (4) one very large grey moth, apparently in a shawl, who appears by her anxiety to be endeavouring to see if there really is a large barrel of butter hidden behind the counter for regular customers only or not. All these are on the outside of my windy pane, drawn to the light because I have not closed the shutters. It's a black night, calm and with a great sweeping sound of sea.

VOL. I

. . . IT'S a divinely beautiful day—so was yesterday. The sky is as blue as the sky can be. I shall go to the Luxembourg gardens this afternoon and count dahlia and baby heads. The Paris gardens are simply a glorious sight with flowers —masses of beloved Japonica, enough Japonica at last. I *shall* have a garden one day, and work in it, too. Plant, weed, tie up, throw over the wall. And the peony border really will be staggering. Oh, how I love flowers ! I think of them with such longing. I go through them, one after another, remembering them from their first moments with love—oh, with rapture, as if they were babies—perhaps. Oh, Earth ! Lovely, unforgettable Earth. Yesterday, I saw the leaves falling, so gently, so softly, raining down from little slender trees, golden against the blue. Perhaps Autumn is loveliest.

VOL. II

NOVEMBER

November. *Set Crab Tree stocks to graft on. In the old of the Moon set Pease and Beans, and sow Parsnips and Carrots, Trench Gardens for Dung, uncover the Roots of your Apple Trees and so let them remain until* March. *Kill Swine in or near the Full of the Moon and the flesh will better prove in Boiling.*

The best Physick this Month is good exercise, warmth, and wholesome Meat and Drink : But if any distemper afflict the body, finish your Physick this Month, and so rest till March, *unless necessity urge. Use good Meat and wholesome Drinks to nourish the Blood. Be sure to go dry of your feet ; for if you go wet of your feet (unless it be those always used to it) be certain to be troubled with Rheume and Cold, and other inconveniences attending.*

British Merlin, 1677

ONE night I was coming back on the last train from London, in a carriage with a woman who was surrounded by billowing yards of new canvas. She was working at one corner in *petit-point* using neutral-coloured wool, and the speed at which she worked amazed me. We talked, of course, and never has a journey gone more quickly. She was an expert, and the work she was just beginning was the first of a set of chairs in *petit-point* in French eighteenth-century style tapestry. During her career she had done embroidery for some of the Royal houses, and during that day she had been meeting a group of women from America, where the interest in embroidery is wider than it is here at present. As I listened to her and thought of my own efforts I realised what a distance lay between us, but we had common ground on one matter. I told her that I wished more women would try to invent designs for themselves, for too many of them, who had a genuine love for embroidery, went into shops and bought ready-made articles with a design stamped on them.

'The lady in the crinoline,' she said, 'I know.'

'And even when they get a stage beyond that,' I said, 'they get stuck with Jacobean designs which though very beautiful have no original conception about them.'

'The difficulty when you start being original,' she said, 'is that amateurs will not cover the work sufficiently with the design they choose. It's a help if you are trying to do this, to make a sketch of the whole—just a rough one, and then, if the subject is floral, put one flower in place of another, in fact try out the whole thing, put some of your own ideas into it, placing your silks or wools in bunches on the places where they will be used. Study some of the old pieces of embroidery in the museums and you'll see what I mean by filling the design.'

I asked her if she tried to vary designs herself, and she said she always did unless she was carrying out a commission to match chairs or stools or hangings.

'And you must remember,' she said, 'that if you are copying an old piece of work the colours you choose should be matched to the colours on the back of the old piece. It's no good starting an elaborate piece of *petit-point* in faded greens and faint rose. It will soon fade to complete drabness. And be adventurous with colours. Remember a solid block of colour is dull. Don't be in-discriminating, but do try to vary your light and shade. Some of the best pieces have half a dozen shades in one leaf. The trick is to decide how the imaginary light falls, and keep the lighter tones on the side nearest to it.'

By the time we parted I had heard fascinating details of how she used human hair for embroidery, and of how one girl she knew, who had long Titian-red hair, said that being friends with an embroideress meant that you would be bald before you were forty! I learnt, too, how she had once lost a great international prize because the strawberry in her Jacobean design had seeds, and no strawberries had seeds before that date.

Since that conversation I have thought a great deal about this business of design; and tried to imagine how some of the oldest and loveliest designs could be adapted for modern use. The point about embroidery today is that it just must be good. The slovenly lazy-daisy stitch, the conventional ready-stamped design are not of much use in a world which has practically discarded mats, except for dinner, embroidered cushions, sachets of all kinds. What we do do must be so good that it can be permanently on show. Embroidery pictures are lovely if the design has been taken from something that stands by itself as a delightful picture. In fact in some of the great embroidery schools a painted design is the first thing on which a student sets to work. She decides on the stitches she will use herself. This suggests at once a whole world of possibilities. Needlework always has been one of the most creative arts since the women of the Stone Age used an awl-like instrument of bone for piercing holes in skins so that they could be joined together by thin strips of leather.

I was looking through a fascinating book called *Needlework Through the Ages*, by May Symonds (Mrs Guy Antrobus) and Louisa Preece, which in the late nineteen twenties was dedicated to Queen Mary. I expect this work is out of print at present, but perhaps your reference library has a copy. If so you can spend some delightful hours with it. Looking through these pages one feels inspired to start adapting at once some of these ancient designs, which would fit so beautifully into our homes where simplicity allied with contrasting richness of tone is the effect we try to produce. Four or five centuries B.C., for instance, a woman embroidered a linen hanging in coloured wool in tones of green, blue and red. There, rescued from an old tomb, is the pattern of little trees, bordered with vines springing from baskets and vases. It has a fresh gaiety and charm even now, and would be so easy to copy that I imagined it used with excellent effect on a bedspread with an embroidered head-board to match. I have never managed to achieve a head-board yet, but I am always choosing designs which I intend to use some day. A great rampant dragon, embroidered in Turkestan in the ninth century in satin, stem and chain stitches of pale yellow and two shades of green, could be used either as a wall picture lit from below, or as a head-board for a man's bed.

I could see a set of most beautiful dinner mats when I looked at the octagonal panels, about 4 inches in diameter, which each showed a device taken from the herbal books of the seventeenth century. The designs in these, except for the Latin names which ran round each border, were almost modern in their clarity and simplicity.

If you are keen to make your own designs, a study of the seventeenth- and eighteenth-century stomachers would give you plenty of ideas. The amount of space for the designs on these was small, of course, and therefore not so intimidating for a beginner. Although small they were nearly always beautifully designed—worked as all good designs must be from the inside out. My favourite stomacher—again I can see it and another like it, for head-boards—was dated 1709. It showed a man and a woman facing each other with showers of lovely flowers and birds falling about them.

In the fifteenth century the Italians made many beautiful running borders of silk embroidery which repay study. Look out for these, and translate the huntsmen, the hounds and the trees into modern idiom. You can do a personal history of your family in embroidery after this manner, but you will do it with greater success if you study the old embroideries which attempted the same thing.

One of the loveliest and most livable rooms I have seen was book-lined except for spaces for huge windows and for some flower pictures. One was a modern flower painting after the manner of Matthew Smith, and the others, about eight of them, were grouped together over a mantlepiece. They were all copies of old flower paintings—each walnut frame showed one flower only, a carnation, a daffodil, a clump of polyanthus, a tea rose—and they were all embroidered in delicate stitches on very fine yellow silk. They were very lovely because none of the thin purity of line which was so characteristic of the old paintings had been lost. It is no good copying something very fine with two or three strands of silk, or blocking all the petals solidly. Using a suitable background, the old paintings can be translated into embroidery if the colours are suggested by delicate stitches, and the groundwork of the petals is not entirely covered.

Tracings of many of these old designs can be taken very easily. A tissue-paper, or, if the design is very bold and clear, a grease-proof paper, tracing can be transferred to the material you have chosen by going over the design again with a piece of carbon paper underneath it.

Even if you are not good at drawing you can enlarge a design by dividing your copy into squares, and then dividing your material into the same number of squares and drawing what appears in each of the same squares in the larger ones.

A piece of the Bayeux tapestry was beautifully enlarged for me in this way, and it has been both an exciting and an amusing thing to do. This piece of embroidery comes into the category of slavish copying, I'm afraid, but now I have done this, and now that I have explored so much further the possibilities of making my own designs I am ambitious to try something more difficult. This small piece of Bayeux tapestry has been delightful to do, partly because in it one has the satisfactory feeling that the designer was a great artist. His groups are combined skilfully with all sorts of decorative conventions—trees and horses and animals—and the stitching is simple and effective. The stitches used are partly outline or stem stitch, partly laid work. There is some reason to believe that the tapestry, which of course is not tapestry at all, but embroidery on linen, was made in England, for in the eleventh century the art of embroidery was further advanced in England than elsewhere, and so many of these designs resemble contemporary English book illustrations.

It is now, of course, among the treasures of the Bayeux Museum, though it has had various adventures during wars, including two trips to Paris, one in 1803 when Napolean had it brought there, no doubt as part of his preliminary publicity campaign for the invasion of England. In 1944 it was exhibited in the Louvre in Paris. A complete set of coloured photographs, the size of the original, are normally on exhibition in the Victoria and Albert Museum.

If you feel you would like to copy a part of this beautiful and romantic piece of embroidery there is an excellent King Penguin which gives you many close-up reproductions of figures so that you may see the stitches.

Another fascinating adventure in embroidery is to copy an old map and use it either as a wall picture, or, as I propose to do some time, a set of dinner mats, or, again as I propose to do some time, a design to put behind a sheet of glass to form part of a guest's bed table. How pleasant to have your toast and coffee and orange juice brought up on a map of the place where you have come to stay. This idea has been commercialised, but it strikes me as being one any embroideress could easily improve on for herself. Again, copies of old maps of the district can nearly always be seen at your local reference library, and among them you are certain to find one that is old and beautiful, and which will be simple enough for you to copy. Many of the seventeenth-century embroidered maps were in *petit-point*, the whole surface being worked, but they respond very well to outline treatment with an assortment of stitches for trees, churches and windmills. If you are really ingenious and greatly prefer contemporary design to any other, you can, by using a good ordnance survey map of your district, make a map which gives special prominence to all the things in which your family are interested. The schools, the church, the playing-fields, your own road, the houses and gardens of your friends can all be put in. You can study some of the old pictorial maps, particularly those of Speed, to see how it was done.

Some time, and I hope it won't be too long before I manage it, I want to make a set of four mats—the big place mats roughly 12 by 16 inches, which are really more use than the very small ones for dinner—of four old maps. One is a coloured and detailed map of Essex by John Oliver (1696). The cartouche in this map is inscribed 'To the Nobility and Gentry of Essex.' Under this high-sounding dedication cherubs are riding on dolphins. Another is Speed's map of Essex divided into hundreds with houses and churches all facing front. A third is Ridler's map of Essex for 1590. Again there are cherubs in the cartouche, apparently doing a little land surveying, and one of the prettiest fleets of ships imaginable sailing away over Oceanus Germanicus. The fourth is a road map, made by John Ogilvy in the seventeenth century, showing the road from London to Harwich. The whole road is put in sections as a ribbon which goes in straight loops up and down the page.

Another source of inspiration for designs is the stone-work on old houses and in cathedrals. These respond very well to embroidery treatment, and are often produced in detail in guide books or on postcards. If you are a good photographer, you can take views of stonework you particularly like and have them enlarged.

And after all this perhaps you will sigh and say, 'If only I hadn't so much mending to do I could perhaps attempt things like that.' The point is you'll do the mending a great deal more efficiently and quickly if you have a piece of work on hand in which you are interested, and which uses your creative faculty to some advantage. Nobody goes on treasuring the socks you have darned, but a really beautiful piece of embroidery may easily become a precious family possession.

A GUY FAWKES PARTY

If the children attending your firework party are very small and their parents must go home early with them, it is not possible to have much in the way of supper. The best idea is to decorate your table with long strands of ivy—it is lovely and shining at this time of the year—and put in the middle a big bowl of rosy apples. Let them be as shiny and eye-catching as possible. Sausage rolls, gingerbread men, conspirator biscuits, and toffee are good things to have to eat, and perhaps ginger beer or hot orange to drink.

If the children are older and everybody can stay later, then you can have more to eat, but stick to traditional food so that it is not quite like other parties. Stuffed baked potatoes are good—that is baked and split and filled with cheese and celery—or a *vol-au-vent* mixture of chopped chicken or meat in a good white sauce. Brandy snaps filled with cream, chestnut tart—a flan filled with chestnut purée and decorated—gingerbread men, and of course apples, and a lot of home-made toffee.

If you are having old English Punch for the grown-ups (and though expensive this is worth it), you can make an imitation punch bowl for the children by heating their orange or lemon drink and floating cherries and slices of orange on top.

Here is the recipe for old English Punch :

Rub the rind of a lemon on a quarter of a pound of loaf sugar. Dissolve the sugar in boiling water, then add half a pint of boiling ale, a gill of strong hot tea, the juice of a lemon and a wineglass each of brandy and rum. Mix well, and serve very hot in a large bowl. These quantities have to be adjusted to the number of guests you have. We multiplied the above quantities by four for a party of about eight.

Lamb's Wool is another good warming drink :

Heat one quart of ale, quarter of a nutmeg grated and one stick of cinnamon, half a teaspoonful of ginger and one pint of sweet white wine, add to four baked apples masked with brown sugar. Strain, reheat and serve.

The mud will be easier to clean off the carpet in the morning.

DECIDING WHETHER YOU CAN EAT THE MUSHROOMS WHICH GROW IN THE GARDEN

THERE may be some people who can adopt a firm confident air towards mushrooms. I wish I were one of them. I think as a nation we must be singularly timid about this food. The most revolting, copper-green and spotted, scarlet and frilled monstrosities are eaten with pleasure and profit by people on the Continent.

Every year out come the mushroom books, and we toy a little with this delightful form of gamble. 'If they don't kill the French they won't kill us,' somebody says, and everybody agrees that this is true, while inwardly reserving the right to believe that English and French stomachs are constructed on entirely different lines.

Roddy is always smitten with apprehension when walking with us in the autumn. 'Mushroom poisoning gives you a revolting death,' he points out, when he sees us picking up a doubtful specimen. 'You die in horrible agony.' Once in the mushroom season he was heard to remark, 'If you two die then I won't get anything. Richard will get whatever you've got, but I think I might have the sports equipment, don't you?'

The Most Disliked Job of the Month—November

When people are trying to be helpful about picking mushrooms, their advice is apt to be either shrouded in superstitions to do with silver spoons, quarters of the moon or tree roots, or else briskly factual and scientific. I think the second sort of advice is harder to bear than the first. The people who give it look at you, when you express doubt as to your ability to tell an edible mushroom from the other kind, with amazement :

'It's quite simple,' they say. 'You just have to be sure they are not the Deathcap—*Amanita Phalloides*—or the Fly Ageric—*Amanita Muscaria*. Avoid those and you can't go wrong.'

'But I don't know how to avoid those,' you say.

'Oh, well, then you'd better not pick mushrooms at all,' they say.

Every year beautiful mushrooms come up in our garden, and every year we are told by at least six people that we are idiots not to eat them, and by six more that we had better have nothing to do with them.

Last year, after hearing from a mushroom expert that they were horse mushrooms and quite definitely edible, Charles and I had some with bacon for breakfast and enjoyed them. We felt pleased to have come to such a pleasant decision on a matter which worried us every autumn. Of course the expert had warned us that not *everybody* could eat horse mushrooms.

I evidently could, but that evening Charles did not want anything to eat, and went on feeling like that for a day or two.

Now the yearly problem must be solved again. Next year do I eat quantities of horse mushrooms alone, or do I make them into ketchup, and if I do will I upset the entire family ?

CONSPIRATOR BISCUITS

THESE have been greatly enjoyed at a Guy Fawkes party, and, I think, are an improvement on gingerbread men. You can, with a little patience, make the conspirators out of the biscuit dough yourself. Use a very sharp-pointed knife. Tall hats, cloaks and two feet at the bottom. Good if you have enough patience left after cooking to add a face by using an icing tube, with white icing and folds of chocolate icing for the cloaks. They look good arranged on a long tray. If you cannot bear to make men, the dough is nice made into tiny rounds filled with butter icing, either coffee or chocolate.

Ingredients

8 *oz. Margarine*	8 *oz. Self-raising flour*
4 *oz. Sugar (castor)*	2 *oz. Powdered chocolate*

Method

Cream butter, beat in sugar ; work in chocolate and flour by degrees. Roll out fairly thinly and cut into shapes. Cook in a moderate oven for twelve minutes.

VISIT TO AN ART GALLERY

PEOPLE who have little to do with children are always amazed at their good taste. If you let them hear good music, see good pictures, films and plays from an early age they will nearly always respond. Their natural taste is usually good, and practically always catholic. I like if I can to look at only a few pictures with them at a time, so that they remember those they do see clearly. Somebody once said of museums and art galleries that they were full of people wandering madly about. The eye can take in only so much, and the feet even less. If you have a good gallery in your town you are fortunate, for you can often drop in with a child to see a favourite picture. If you are in London with a child try and look at some of the Dutch interiors in the National Gallery. Children always like the serenity and reassurance of these, the polished details and the pictures within pictures which Jan Vermeer, Peter de Hooch, Michael Sweerts and Jan Steen loved to paint.

If the great masterpieces seem too big for a child to appreciate, as indeed they nearly always are, it is easy enough in the National Gallery to pick out in many pictures an animal or a child which will, later, send them back to discover the beauty of the whole for themselves. Illustrating this point is the little dog in *Giovanni Arnoldfini* by Van Eyck ; the magnificent dragon in Tintoretto's *St George and the Dragon* ; the ox and the ass in Botticelli's *The Nativity* ; the most lovable lion in Filippo Lippi's *St Jerome* ; the child skaters in Hendrik Avercamp's *Winter Scene* ; and the little girl with a hoop in Renoir's *Les Parapluies*.

The great Uccello masterpiece, *The Rout of San Romano*, with its wonderful composition of horses, banners, pikes and flowering hedges, is really enough for one visit for a child who really looks at it, and they usually do. The same can be said for the calm architectural Canalettos.

At the Tate Gallery there are the modern pictures which most children have grown familiar with at school, at home, and in shops which sell modern reproductions. There are the paintings of Cezanne, Van Gogh, Monet and Paul Nash. While children love the brilliance, the clarity, the sense of sun imprisoned in these, the impressionist nature of these pictures makes them more difficult to grasp.

ELIZABETH AND HER GERMAN GARDEN

It takes a long time to make my spring lists. I want to have a border all yellow, every shade of yellow from fieriest orange to nearly white, and the amount of work and studying of gardening books it costs me will only be appreciated by beginners like myself. I have been weeks planning it, and it is not nearly finished. I want it to be a succession of glories from May till the frosts, and the chief feature is to be the number of 'ardent marigolds'—flowers that I very tenderly love—and nasturtiums. The nasturtiums are to be of every sort and shade, and are to climb and creep and grow in bushes, and show their lovely flowers and leaves to the best advantage. Then there are to be eschscholtzias, dahlias, sunflowers, zinnias, scabiosa, portulaca, yellow violas, yellow stocks, yellow sweet peas, yellow lupins—everything that is yellow or that has a yellow variety. The place I have chosen for it is a long wide border in the sun, at the foot of a grassy slope crowned with lilacs and pines, and facing south-east. You go through a little pine wood, and, turning a corner, are to come suddenly upon this bit of captured morning glory. I want it to be blinding in its brightness after the dark cool path through the wood.

EMMA

Upon such occasions poor Mr Woodhouse's feelings were in sad warfare. He loved to have the cloth laid, because it had been the fashion of his youth, but his conviction of suppers being very unwholesome made him rather sorry to see anything put on it ; and while his hospitality would have welcomed his visitors to everything, his care for their health made him grieve that they would eat.

Such another small basin of thin gruel as his own was all that he could, with thorough self-approbation, recommend ; though he might constrain himself, while the ladies were comfortably clearing the nicer things, to say :

'Mrs Bates, let me propose your venturing on one of these eggs. An egg boiled very soft is not unwholesome. Serle understands boiling an egg better than anybody. I would not recommend an egg boiled by anybody else—but you need not be afraid, they are very small, you see—one of our small eggs will not hurt you. Miss Bates, let Emma help you to a *little* bit of tart—a *very* little bit. Ours are all apple tarts. You need not be afraid of unwholesome preserves here. I do not advise the custard. Mrs Goddard, what say you to *half* a glass of wine ? A *small* half-glass, put into a tumbler of water ? I do not think it could disagree with you.'

Emma allowed her father to talk—but supplied her visitors in a much more satisfactory style.

JANE AUSTEN

DECEMBER

December. *In the last Quarter of the Moon, this Month and the next, are the best times to fell Timber : let Fowlers mind their game. Cover all your best flowers and herbs from cold and storm with rotten Horse-dung. Look well to thy cattle, Blood horses. Let a warm fire, and a cup of* Nectar *be thy Bath ; the Kitchen thy Apothecaries Shop, hot Meats and Broths thy Physick, and a well spred Table the Proof of thy Charity to thy poor Neighbours to whom this avice is seasonable :*

If thou be poor, and canst not feast at all,
Thank God for such as thee to feasting call.

The best Physick is as befor, a merry honest heart, and the exercise of charity among thy poor neighbours. The next year I will commend those who keep good Houses this year.

British *Merlin*, 1677

THE DRESSING-UP BOX

PARTICULARLY in these days when Cecil B. de Mille and others allow us at the cost of 2s 6d or less to dress up vicariously as often as we wish, a dressing-up box is a good family possession. Just because it is so easy to watch people from six to sixty perfectly groomed in every kind of fancy dress on television or at the cinema, any simple creative effort on the part of the family becomes more valuable.

You may watch, on a screen, a skilled Indian snake charmer, and yawn in the middle of his act, but you laugh and go on laughing when you find your younger son sitting on the floor with a dinner napkin wound into a turban, and his white shirt floating outside his trousers, piping a tune to the black coils of the Hoover extension.

You want both sorts of entertainment. You get the first anyway. A dressing-up box makes the second easier.

Also, believe me, at Christmas there is no better way of providing an adult recovery period than giving the children *carte blanche* with a box of clothes.

Put the box in a well-warmed room away from you—see the fire is well guarded—and on a wet afternoon, or in the middle of a party you may not see them for a blissful half-hour. They will be happy and entertained, and at the end you will be strong enough to endure, and even to appreciate, the charade or play.

The difficulty about the presentation of a family effort is usually the stage. In our house, early Victorian and possessing that marvel of its period a 'withdrawing room' with double doors, replaced by curtains now, we have an almost perfect stage with its own side entrance. But this is distinctly unusual, and delightful though it is we pay for it in the matter of draughts. Where the fire is, there will my heart be also, is apt to be the Englishman's motto in his chilly home.

All but the youngest and least self-conscious of the performers are apt to feel the disadvantage of trooping in before an audience blasé and chocolate eating, and sunk deeply in armchairs, without the mystery-providing curtain. So there must be a curtain of sorts.

If you have screens to partition off the space round the door, that is well enough, provided the screens are not too tall and apt to crash down on the audience if handled by people of four foot something. If you have no screen, blankets draped over the obiquitous clothes horse, or, if the children must have glamour, beflowered bedspreads or curtains, are perfect. A three-fold clothes horse is best of all.

As to what is in the box, a collection which grows un-self-consciously is better in the end than one which is too ambitiously period. Anybody who has sufficient money can buy elaborate costumes, but these have no personal significance, and can never produce those moments of delicious reminiscing which make the inclined-to-be-long intervals less long in a home-produced play.

'You saw the pink evening frock Charlotte was wearing, I like those sleeves even now, don't you? I was wearing that frock the night of the fire—that mend at the back is where it got caught on the drainpipe.'

By the time you've heard about the fire the second act is ready to start.

I always regret one set of sombre widow's weeds I was not allowed to put into the dressing-up box.

I suppose I was about twelve when a friend and I played what became known as the weeping-widow hoax on my father.

'There is a poor woman in black in the hall, Daddy. She's crying, and she wants to see you.'

Ominous words to a kind-hearted parson who could never refuse anything, even if it were asked for without tears.

I can still see my father's hand go to his pocket as he left the study and walked down the hall to where the slim figure in black stood silhouetted against the light which flooded in from the garden and the sun-dazzled Cornish sea.

The weeping widow was a boarding-school friend, and I had dressed her up in the black clothes which had come from London in a big crate. The Cornish tin mines were going through a period of acute depression, mines were closing, and charitable people in London were sending clothes to Cornwall. The rich widow's weeds, early Edwardian and terrifyingly stiff, my mother had put aside as unlikely to cheer any miner's wife at the moment, but as possibly useful later, and we had found them.

As soon as my father and the widow started to talk I rushed upstairs to hide my laughter and to tell my mother, and we both hung over the bannisters.

'I don't think its very kind,' my mother whispered; 'you know how he suffers for people—and listen, she's got six children. His heart will be bleeding!'

'It's only for a minute,' I reassured her.

My father's hand had come out of his pocket now, and he was guiding the heavily veiled figure to the dining-room.

'Come and sit down,' he was saying, 'and I'll ask my wife about some clothes for those children. And you must have some tea.'

This was complete triumph, so complete that I was rather regretting it, and I rushed down to meet him.

'I haven't seen this Mrs Trepiddick before,' he was saying, 'but she seems to be in great trouble. All her children are boys, and shortage of trousers seems to be the difficulty.' And then he added, seeing our faces, 'Is it funny ? You don't usually laugh at cases like this ! '

At that moment there was a rush of feet along the passage, a smell of moth ball, and the sobbing widow, with her veil thrown back and her rosy thirteen-year-old face full of concern, launched herself on my father, holding out the money and apologising for having wrung his heart.

'I didn't know I'd got such talent as an actress,' she said. 'I shall go on to the stage when I grow up. That's decided. But I'd never have done it if I thought I could take you in so well.'

My mother was quite deaf to our plea that the weeds would be wonderful for reading-the-will scenes, and murder plays, and that no real widow of today would wear them. That wasn't the point, she said, somebody might be glad to have them, and before long somebody was.

A Victorian christening cloak of scarlet and cream cashmere, tasselled and quite hideous, is now one of the chief treasures in our dressing-up box. In the beginning it must have spread a militant patch of colour across the virtuous façade of either mother or nurse, the colour inspired perhaps by the notable behaviour of the baby's father in a far-flung battlefield. In the end it still supplies glory. Moths have feasted modestly from the cream padding here and there, but the general appearance is still reminiscent of bugles and Buckingham Palace, pageantry and Poona. I don't think the present generation connect it with babies at all, but it is regularly used as a highwayman's cloak, an apron when the scene is domestic, for little Red Riding Hood, a saddle cloth for an emperor's horse, a flag to attract passing vessels hung from a raft in mid-Atlantic, or part of Queen Boadicea's chariot ensemble. And note that the woman who, a hundred years or so, ago sewed the satin strings on must have been a person with long-distance views. After all this they still show no signs of coming off.

We have not many such period pieces in our box. If one has a great-great aunt who kept in the attic a trunk full of her great-grandmother's clothes, and one day hands them over to you, then that is a gift from heaven, of course, but don't add too many contemporary clothes to a dressing-up box. They are apt to be dreary and bulky, apt to attract moths, and take far too long to obtain vintage value. This does not apply to evening dresses, but to almost everything else—except old suede or leather golfing jackets, degree or students' gowns, hoods and mortar boards. Two of the regular favourites in our box are a 1920-5 gold evening frock with large pink roses *appliquéd* on the skirt, and a suede golf jacket. The first is invariably used to suggest high life, the second low—usually something of the Brighton Rock variety, with a touch of Wild West in the accompanying fringed trousers. Japanese kimonos are always useful too, but I do not recommend old dressing-gowns, unless you have a crimson one in the family, useful for Father Christmas and mediaeval characters and coronation scenes.

The war years, when it was necessary to make most presents for the boys, added some valuable props to our box.

One year, driven to desperation by empty shops in which nothing appeared except giraffes made out of blue checked gingham, and battleships of badly glued oblongs of grey wood, I made two Red Indian suits and a wigwam for Roddy and Richard. The suits were dark brown and of boiler-suit material, so that they are not only with us yet but look like being appreciated by the grandchildren—if any. On the sleeves were embroidered in simple outline various tribal emblems, red antlers, a brown owl, acorns, trees, etc.

The wigwam was of rust-red hessian, and the feathered head-dresses, truly magnificent, the product of every farmyard we knew, the feathers being home-dyed or painted. These costumes come out all the year round and are often borrowed. The trousers, heavily fringed, are, like mackintoshes, hardly ever out of use. The head-dresses were unfortunately stolen from a hat box in a carrier's cart. I only hope the person who stole them gave them to children who really appreciated them.

Once the Red Indian ensemble provided an idea for a winter birthday party for young children. The wigwam was erected in a clear space, and a mock fire made before it of small logs and red papers and a torch or two. Spruce boughs, propped against what furniture had to remain, provided an illusion of a forest, and the feast was spread on coloured rugs. The hosts in full Indian costume, doled out Indian head-dresses to the visitors, and one way and another, at small cost, there was a satisfactory feeling that foreign parts had been visited. The pipe of peace turned into a soap-bubble session, and that was, if a little out of period, very popular.

It is pleasant if the things in a dressing-up box can be genuine articles rather than copies of things, and there can be no more suitable repository for bright, unusable curiosities bought abroad. In this way they can all be kept together, and will be a recurring joy instead of lurking dingily at the back of drawers and cupboards.

In our box we have a pair of Swiss-Italian *zoccoli*, the heel-less wooden shoes with the velvet straps into which you thrust your feet. I wore these for a few weeks when we returned from Italian Switzerland, but have not worn them since. They are, with the slender red-lined slippers from Jaipur, exquisitely embroidered and toe-upturned, perfect examples of shoes worn by the ordinary people in the places where they were bought. The two Indian hats bought by Charles for the boys are to be seen every day worn by small Muslim boys in Bombay. One of royal purple worked with gold thread is sombrely magnificent, but the bright-red one, wreathed with green and yellow embroidery, is more attractively gay. Set apart in a box is the ceremonial garland sent to me by a South Indian friend, and this adds Eastern glory to any scene. The garland is of gold tinsel, ropes of it, interspersed here and there by velvet plaques. In its bright length are large artificial pearls and pink and green tassels. In an English setting it asks for more glory to be added to it, a sari of gold tissue, and an accompanying wealth of flowers, and what it gets is usually the tarnished-gold evening gown. I only lend my jade-green cashmere shawl on special occasions, but it has already been worn in two plays, outside the family.

Small children do not like masks, usually. They dislike the real eyes in the dead face, and this is instinctively right, I think. The pleasure of horror and grotesquerie is a later development, and some children never acquire it. But plain black highwaymen's masks are a constant pleasure. They don't pretend to be a whole face. To the children they seem attractively wicked, and to the adults there is a distinct pleasure in contemplating three planes—one, the wide and innocent forehead ; two, the sootily-set bright eyes ; three, the pink cheeks and supposedly savage red mouth uttering suitable oaths and threats. Yes, masks are essential, also a box of false moustaches and a beard or two, and some make-up.

Any kind of weapon. We have an interesting old pistol, a sword, and invariably the poker which is an old French bayonet comes into use. Musical instruments, too, tambourines or drums and flutes. One can bear them that long anyway. Feathers and fans, jewellery, filmy scarves and coloured stockings are useful. We had a treasured pair of thick pure silk magenta stockings, and were never tired of speculating about their origin. Who could have wanted such a colour—ever ?

From two wars have been salvaged a blue walking-out uniform jacket, various berets, a Mickey Mouse gas mask, a camouflaged waterproof, an American Mae West, and, from a long-ago affair, a red-coat's bandolier. Whole uniforms are again too bulky, and not to be encouraged. One significant object can, as in modern painting, be used to suggest the whole quite adequately.

I've put down some of the things we have to give the idea of how a dressing-up box arrives. If you have a big trunk which you are unlikely to use again, or a big laundry basket which can be kept in a cupboard, an attic or nursery, and moved easily at Christmas, then it is likely to repay you many times for the room it takes up by providing a use for all the picturesque oddments accumulating from travels, school plays, fancy-dress parties, dances on liners, and the more solemn events in a family's history—getting a degree, going to a war, being married and even, as in the case of the invaluable christening cloak, being born.

PLANNING A CONTINENTAL HOLIDAY

The criticism that this is not a job, but more a wicked indulgence in fantasy, may be made here, but the fact remains that if you are thinking of going abroad at Easter or in the summer, the thinking must be done in December or you may be too late. And what more delightful, more refreshing, than to sit under the fading greenery of Christmas, and, with the prospect of school-holiday meals solid as a concrete pavement stretching before you, to talk of the tree-shaded bell-loud canals of Bruges, the shell-encrusted water-level rooms of Isola Bella, where the reflections swim like mermaids, or the smell of pine and the crême-de-menthe water frothing under a frieze of flowers in the woods above Lac d'Annecy.

Get if you can at the beginning a *Cook's Continental Time Table*. There is nothing like looking up trains and boats to make the whole proposition come alive.

The Most Disliked Job of the Month—December

MAKING CHILDREN WRITE THANK-YOU LETTERS

THIS is the worst thing. Every year we discuss the possibility of getting out a printed form for the children, tastefully decorated to soften the blow.

Something on these lines :

Dear		
Thank you		most terribly very, very much a lot
for the . . .		
This is/will be		just what I wanted perfectly lovely smashing very good for me
A money present picture book mechanical toy doll gloves talcum powder soap	*is*	what I like best the root of all evil smashing absolutely thrilling an insult

Love,
Yours/Yours sincerely,

* *Cross out words which do not apply*

The Most Disliked Job of the Month—December

Yes, we think about it every year, talk of it, usually when we're watching a rebellious and ink-stained recipient of a delightful present breathing heavily over a writing pad.

Bitter yearly query :

' The cave men didn't write. Who invented writing ? '

And how much worse is the thank-you process whether done by self or offspring when, as on one Christmas morning, Roddy opened all his presents and sat in the middle of them firing a pop-gun, and nobody had the slightest idea which gift tag belonged to which present.

TRAVELLER'S PIE

ON Christmas Eve everybody is apt to be either a traveller or one who receives travellers, and whichever you are, to nibble a leaf of lettuce because tomorrow you are going to eat rather more than usual is to ensure that depression sets in long before you are allowed to go to bed.

If children are involved in your house party Christmas Eve is, besides being the nicest, perhaps the most exhausting night of the year. You'll be able to stand on ladders, stop children from asking if it's morning, or eel your way into the blackest depths of the shoe cupboard where the model railway was hidden back in August, and, if you're a guest, help your host and hostess to do these things with more Yuletide eagerness, if your evening meal has been moderately earthy rather than spiritual in tone.

The joy of this meal is that it can be prepared long before, and you need not make your guests uneasy by appearing exhausted by the first round.

Therefore Traveller's Pie.

Recipe

1½ lb. Stewing steak	*4 Shallots (optional)*
Sheep's kidneys	*Some sliced potatoes*
2 Hardboiled eggs (optional)	*A little paprika*

Puff Pastry

½ lb. Flour	*Salt*
½ lb. Lard and margarine mixed	*Water*

Method

Cut the steak and kidney into small inviting pieces, removing all skin and gristle and fat, and core from kidneys. Roll the meat in seasoned flour and place in a pie dish. If you wish to cook the steak in a casserole first so as to be sure it is tender, that is quite a good idea. It is important for the pie to be large and festive looking, and not inclined to deflate in the middle, so judicious padding may be done with sliced potato as a foundation. Add some water, and boil up the discarded bits separately so you can add some liquid later in the cooking through a funnel. Sprinkling of chopped shallots and paprika, and eggs as lightly boiled as will peel without breaking, are the grace notes of the composition.

Short crust is very suitable, but puff pastry more exciting.

LUNCH AT A DICKENSIAN INN

COME to it, please, if you can, after a walk in the wind, or on a day of snapping cold. Do not just drive there in the car. And make it after Christmas when you feel that if you have to produce another meal you will laugh hysterically and go out into the garden and start cropping grass.

Dickensian Inns, because Dickens seems to have put his own mark of joviality on inns and Christmas generally. When one passes the White Horse Inn at Ipswich, or the Angel at Bury St Edmunds, somebody murmurs : 'Yes, of course Pickwick stayed there,' and that, as far as most English people, and many Americans, are concerned, has now become an established fact. It has more reality than the accurate statement that the White Horse and the Angel were there long before Dickens was able to hold a pen.

There are not many places in England, except those remote in themselves, out of reach of an inn where it is possible to have a well-cooked, and sometimes, even in these days, a superlative meal, in surroundings of such interest that the whole family remembers the outing, and, moreover, gets a feeling of the history of the town or village in which the inn is set. Very often the inn is the oldest thing in the town, older even than the church, and tracing the various signs of its history can be as interesting as reading a detective story.. How very soon the children respond to the stimulus of a ghost story like this:

'A well-known actress was woken from sleep in her room in a Bristol inn recently by the sensation that feet, heavy top-booted feet, were passing through her body, and going up over her head into the wall. The first time this happened she thought it was a nightmare, but on the second night, when it happened in exactly the same way, she asked about the history of the inn, and found that many years before a small winding staircase from the yard occupied the corner of the room exactly where the bed was, and was much used by ostlers and coachmen.'

When the delicious significance of this has been absorbed, half an hour before lunch will fly past while the family looks at the inn yard—if your inn is fortunately one of those which has a yard—with eyes which really see things. They will search for signs of old staircases, mark that there was once a bedroom gallery, now fronted with glass, and that the grill room had a row of mangers. Somebody with a really quick eye finds out that the attractive regular pattern of beams on the long wall of the grill room was part of the woodwork at the back of the loose boxes.

Why, somebody is sure to ask, do you so often see old playbills framed in the entrances to inns? Quite often the playbills go with an inn which has a good yard, and then it is easy enough to see how the yard was always used as a theatre by the travelling players, and how the modern theatre is in a way the large flourishing baby, architecturally, of the old inn yard.

And there are inn signs. Richard and Roddy are knowledgable now about wrought iron, and on car journeys point out good examples of supports. Quite often these remain when the signs themselves are destroyed, or replaced by modern productions of doubtful merit. But if the inn sign is interesting ask the landlord about it. Like a good host, he is pleased to talk of his home and the delightful things in it, and more often than not there's an excellent story attached to the inn sign.

One could go on for ever, for the possibilities of an hour or so in a good inn are infinite. We, as a family, are fortunate, for inns of distinct quality are within walking distance of home. One can, and most of us do, use the yard of one of them as a short cut. The Red Lion's foundations date back to 1470, but heaven knows what bulgings and stretchings, what infinite variety of alterations and rebuildings have gone on since then. And what was it before it was an inn ? The fragment of Roman paving, displayed behind glass opposite you as you sip your sherry, speaks for itself, or nearly does.

A visit to an inn can be made the focal point of a whole day of the Christmas holidays, and provide entertainment and speculation for most of it. And from your personal point of view the very fact of having the modern equivalents of neat's tongue, roast swan, venison, lampreys, saffron cake, marchpane and citrons in picturesque surroundings is a relaxation.

CHRISTMASSE-EVE. ANOTHER CEREMONIE

Come guard this night the Christmas-pie,
That the thiefe, though ne'r so slie,
With his flesh-hooks, don't come nie
    To catch it.

From him, who all alone sits there,
Having his eyes still in his eare,
And a deale of nightly feare
    To watch it.

THOMAS TUSSER, 1531

WUTHERING HEIGHTS

CATHY stayed at Thrushcross Grange five weeks, till Christmas. . . . Instead of a wild hatless little savage jumping into the house, and rushing to squeeze us all breathless, there alighted from a handsome black pony a very dignified person with brown ringlets falling from the cover of a feathered beaver, and a long cloth habit, which she was obliged to hold up with both hands that she might sail in.

She gently kissed me ; I was in flour, making the Christmas cake, and it would not have done to give me a hug ; and then she looked round for Heathcliff.

Heathcliff was hard to discover at first. If he were careless and uncared for before Catherine's absence, he had been ten times more so since.

Nobody but I even did him the kindness to call him a dirty boy, and bid him wash himself once a week ; and children of his age seldom have a natural pleasure in soap and water. Therefore, not to mention his clothes, which has seen three months' service in mire and dust, and his thick uncombed hair, the surface of his face and hands were dismally beclouded. He might well skulk behind the settle, on beholding such a bright graceful damsel enter the house, instead of a rough-headed counterpart of himself, as he expected. . . .

Cathy, catching a glimpse of her friend in his concealment, flew to embrace him ; she bestowed seven or eight kisses on his cheek within the second, and then stopped, and drawing back, burst into a laugh, exclaiming :

'Why, how very black and cross you look ! and how—how funny and grim ! . . .

She had some reason to put the question, for shame and pride threw double gloom over his countenance, and kept him immoveable.

'Shake hands, Heathcliff,' said Mr Earnshaw condescendingly ; 'once in a way, that is permitted.'

'I shall not,' replied the boy, finding his tongue at last ; 'I shall not stand to be laughed at. I shall not bear it ! '

And he would have broken from the circle, but Miss Cathy seized him again.

'I did not mean to laugh at you,' she said ; 'I could not hinder myself ; Heathcliff, shake hands at least ! What are you sulky for ? It was only that you looked odd. If you wash your face and brush your hair, it will be all right ; but you are so dirty ! '

'You needn't have touched me ! ' he answered, following her eye, and snatching away his hand. 'I shall be as dirty as I please, and I like to be dirty, and I will be dirty.'

With that he dashed head foremost out of the room. . . .

After playing lady's-maid to Cathy and putting my cakes in the oven, and making the house and kitchen cheerful with great fires, befitting Christmas Eve, I prepared to sit down and amuse myself by singing carols all alone ; . . . .

. . . I smelt the rich scent of the heating spices ; and admired the shining kitchen utensils, the polished clock decked in holly, the silver mugs ranged on a tray ready to be filled with mulled ale for supper ; and, above all, the speckless purity of my particular care—the scoured and well-swept floor.

I gave due inward applause to every object, and then I remembered how old Earnshaw used to come in when all was tidied, and call me a cant lass, and slip a shilling into my hand as a Christmas-box ; and from that I went on to think of his fondness for Heathcliff, and his dread lest he should suffer neglect after death had removed him ; and that naturally led me to consider the poor lad's situation now, and from singing I changed my mind to crying. It struck me soon, however, there would be more sense in endeavouring to repair some of his wrongs than shedding tears over them ; I got up and walked into the court to seek him. He was not far ; I found him smoothing the glossy coat of the new pony in the stable, and feeding the other beasts, according to custom.

'Make haste, Heathcliff ! ' I said, ' the kitchen is so comfortable, and Joseph is upstairs ; make haste, and let me dress you smart before Miss Cathy comes out, and then you can sit together, with the whole hearth to yourselves, and have a long chatter till bed-time.'

He proceeded with his task and never turned his head towards me.

'Come—are you coming ? ' I continued. 'There's a little cake for each of you, nearly enough ; and you'll need half an hour's donning.'

EMILY BRONTË

UNDER THE GREENWOOD TREE

It being Christmas day, the tranter prepared himself with Sunday particularity. Loud sousing and snorting noises were heard to proceed from a tub in the back quarters of the dwelling, proclaiming that he was there performing his great Sunday wash, lasting half an hour, to which his washings on working-day mornings were mere flashes in the pan. Vanishing into the outhouse with a large brown towel, and the above-named bubblings and snortings being carried on for about twenty minutes, the tranter would appear round the edge of the door, smelling like a summer fog, and looking as if he had just narrowly escaped a watery grave with the loss of much of his clothes, having since been weeping bitterly till his eyes were red ; a crystal drop of water hanging ornamentally at the bottom of each ear, one at the tip of his nose, and others in the form of spangles about his hair.

Thomas Hardy

CHRISTMAS

Get ivy and hull, woman, deck up thine house,
And take this same brawn for to seethe and to souse ;
Provide us good cheer, for thou knowest the old guise,
Old customs good be, let no man despise.
At Christmas be merry and thank God of all,
And feast thy poor neighbours, the great and the small.
Yea, all the year long have an eye to the poor,
And God shall send luck to keep open thy door.
Good fruit and good plenty do well in thy loft,
Then lay for an orchard and cherish it oft.

The profit is mickle, the pleasure is much ;
At pleasure with profit few wise men will grutch.
For plants and for stocks lay aforehand to cast,
But set or remove them, while Twelve-tide do last.

THOMAS TUSSER, 1531